THE COMPLETE BOOK OF JUDO

GEORGE R. PARULSKI, Jr.

5th DAN

FORMER AAU
CHAMPION

ENDORSED BY:

THE AMERICAN
SOCIETY OF
CLASSICAL JUDOKA

THE ALL-JAPAN
SEIBUKAN MARTIAL
ARTS AND WAYS
ASSOCIATION

Contemporary Books, Inc.
Chicago

Library of Congress Cataloging in Publication Data

Parulski, George R.
   The complete book of judo.

   Bibliography: p.
   Includes index.
   1. Judo.   I. Title.
GV1114.P37   1984   796.8'152   84-4319
ISBN 0-8092-5450-6

DEDICATION

To
Mom and Dad,
who taught me that
the thousand-mile road to true martial art
fulfillment begins with a single step

Published by Contemporary Books, Inc.
180 North Michigan Avenue, Chicago, Illinois 60601
Manufactured in the United States of America
Library of Congress Catalog Card Number: 84-4319
International Standard Book Number: 0-8092-5450-6

Published simultaneously in Canada by Beaverbooks, Ltd.
195 Allstate Parkway, Valleywood Business Park
Markham, Ontario L3R 4T8 Canada

CONTENTS

ACKNOWLEDGMENTS   v

FOREWORD   vii

INTRODUCTION   viii

1. HISTORICAL BACKGROUND   1

2. THEORY   7

3. HOLISTIC CONDITIONING   23

4. NAGE-WAZA *(THROWING TECHNIQUES)*   67

5. KATAME-WAZA *(PINNING, LOCKING, AND CHOKING TECHNIQUES)*   117

6. STRATEGY   135

7. AN AFTERWORD   141

APPENDIX I: *THE RANKING SYSTEM*   143

APPENDIX II: *NUTRITIONAL INFORMATION FOR JUDO TRAINING*   147

APPENDIX III: *INTERNATIONAL JUDO FEDERATION'S RULES OF SPORT JUDO*   154

APPENDIX IV: *THE KATA OF JUDO*   164

APPENDIX V: *GLOSSARY*   167

ABOUT THE AUTHOR   175

ABOUT THE ASSISTANTS   176

END NOTES   177

BIBLIOGRAPHY   178

INDEX   179

ACKNOWLEDGMENTS

My sincere thanks to the following people and organizations for cooperation in completing and preparing this book: Bayview YMCA (Webster, New York) for their support of the Yama-ji and for letting us use their facility for photographic purposes; Carolyn Parulski, my wife, friend, and supporter, who helped me prepare the manuscript and take the photos for the text; Hillside Children's Center, for use of their gymnasium during one of many photo sessions; Bill Rourke and Rob Horowitz, true *judoka* who modeled for many of the pictures in the book; Sensei Obato, president of the American Society of Classical Judoka, for his support in this project; and Ty Brown, black-and-white-processing supervisor for Custom Color Labs (Kansas City), for his care in processing and printing the pictures in this book. Thank you!

FOREWORD

Judo or, more specifically, *kodokan* judo, was founded in 1882 by Dr. Jigoro Kano as a physical and mental training experience. Today it has become an international sport and is practiced according to the same rules everywhere. In addition to its homeland of Japan, judo is extremely popular in Europe and America and is practiced by both men and women equally.

Judo is a modern adaption of *jujutsu*, one of Japan's martial arts of old and a precious legacy of the samurai.

It has been pointed out to me that the need has long existed for a book that shows the complete *gokyu-waza* (forms of throwing, numbering 40) and *katame-waza* (forms of holding) in their traditional light. Two such books, *The Illustrated Kodokan Judo* (Kodansha Publishing) and *Gokyo-waza*, existed, but both have long been out of print. With new generations of *judoka* (judo players) arriving on the scene daily, the need has never been greater.

Several excellent books on judo play are on the market today, the best ones being the *Judo in Action* series, and the *Vital Judo* series (Japan Publications). The former, however, shows only a limited number of judo techniques (not the complete program), and the latter is a very personal interpretation of judo techniques used specifically in competition.

What is needed is a volume that will show *all gokyo* techniques, as well as *katame-waza* in their *traditional* or classic form. This way a student learns the original method first and can build personal interpretation from there. Also, it is necessary to show some modern application of the classical throws, all in a single volume. *The Complete Book of Judo* is such a text.

The author is eminently qualified to write a book of this nature, and with his combined skills of flawless technique, professional photography, and writing, he has created a work to be valued for many years to come.

ISAO OBATO
Sixth-Degree Black Belt
President/Founder
American Society of Classical Judoka
Arizona, June 1983

INTRODUCTION

The scope of judo is vast, perhaps as vast as human culture itself. Judo in essence encompasses so many different aspects that nearly every practitioner would define judo differently.

To some, judo is a sport; to others, an art; and to still others, it is a method of self-defense. As a sport, judo is recognized by the AAU and as such has found a place in the Olympic Games. Nearly every country on the face of this earth has a judo team of some capacity. In the United States, *sport judo*, as we will call it, is a very popular pastime. Many high schools and colleges offer sport judo as an official course; in many universities degree credits can be earned through the study of sport judo.

In this country sport judo is recognized by two main bodies: The United States Judo Association and The United States Judo Federation. However, these organizations represent only the sport of judo, and judo practiced as a way of life or as an *art* has little or no place with them.

Because of this, two new organizations have found their way into the world of judo, one an invention of the United States alone, the other an import from Japan. These two organizations, the Seibu-kan Association (from

Japan) and the American Society of Classical Judoka (American), are gaining more and more acceptance in classical judo circles. What is classical judo? Simply put, it is judo practiced for self-defense and *kata* (art) rather than for competition. The techniques are the same, but the methodology is different. Also, classical judo relies on judo *goshin* (self-defense) and all seven judo *kata* (forms), whereas sport judo relies mainly on who can throw or pin whom first.

First, I should mention that there is nothing wrong with sport judo. In fact, taught properly, it can be a very rewarding experience. My point is simply that there are other types of judo, and one need only open his eyes to find them.

The purpose of this book is to present the sport of judo in the light of classical technique. In my experience, competitive skill is increased severalfold when the traditional methods are adhered to rather than parted from.

Many books on the market give a "champion's" view of how to improve this or that technique. However, unless one learns the classical method first, one can hardly hope to add his own interpretation.

Judo as a sport offers many benefits. As a

contact sport it offers the thrill of wrestling with an even greater challenge. Judo relies more on standing techniques (throws) and requires a greater skill of execution than wrestling. Therefore, as a sport, judo is extremely challenging.

For the quiet, shy person, judo can boost self-confidence. Withdrawn individuals often have no belief in themselves. Judo gives them something to be proud of—something that is very much them.

For the karate or kung fu student, judo offers a degree of self-defense not offered by either of those arts. All too often the *karateka* (karateist) who uses his skills on an attacker damages him more than the law will allow. In karate it is very hard to predict the amount of damage you will inflict on an opponent. But in judo you can control and hold without causing serious injury—an effective alternative for dealing with the drunk who is also your uncle.

As a method of exercise, judo stimulates both aerobic and anaerobic activity within the body, bringing about a high degree of physical fitness. The discipline, self-confidence, and self-control result in a high degree of psychological fitness as well.

Because of this, many consider judo a *holistic* approach to health. I am in perfect agreement with this, and I stress it in my teaching method. Students often refer to my judo as "holistic judo" because I am very concerned about developing the entire person with the whole of judo: art, sport, self-defense. I do this by instructing my students on proper diet and incorporating yoga and meditation into my classes. Over the years many of my competitive students have increased their sport performance greatly with this approach. One went on to win a national AAU title and may even represent the United States in the summer Olympics one day.

Therefore, *The Complete Book of Judo* is written with the holistic approach in mind. I cover traditional warm-ups and conditioning exercises but add a special section on yogic exercises aimed specifically at the *judoka* (judo player). We will discuss diet and nutrition as it relates to a *judoka*'s specific training routine.

We will pull each technique apart by learning judo theories and physics thoroughly. Each throw will be performed at its classic best; but again, with throws most suited for competition I will give a modern approach as well.

It is thus my hope to present judo in a fuller light than it has been to date. I hope that the new material in this book (and the old material that is presented in a fresher, more refined light) will justify your keeping it on your bookshelf. If, from time to time, *The Complete Book of Judo* can help you get over a slump, when you are trying to develop new skills or fresh outlooks, I shall be very pleased.

Where such words exist, I have used the universally accepted Japanese terminology for techniques throughout the text. This practice is intended to create a universal language for the judo practitioner, making it possible to train anywhere in the world and still be understood in the *dojo* (training hall) to a functional degree. However, where there is no traditional terminology for a particular application, I did not take the liberty of devising my own Japanese term (Japanese ideographs are very convenient for doing just that); instead, I used English since I am writing for a predominantly English-speaking readership. (Readers will find a comprehensive list of terms and definitions in the Glossary.)

Finally, it is my hope that this text will help further understanding of the ideal of judo according to Dr. Kano, judo's founder: a method for learning about and improving oneself—mentally, physically, psychologically, and spiritually.

George R. Parulski, Jr.
Fourth-Degree Black Belt
Webster, New York, July 1983

Jigoro Kano, founder of judo (1860–1938).
Photo courtesy Dai-Nippon Seibukan Budo/
Bugei-Kai.

Conclave of leading jujutsu men at the Dai-Nippon Butokukai (All-Japan Martial Arts Hall) in Kyoto on July 24, 1906, to formulate the official *katas* (forms) to be used by *kodokan judoka* (judo men). Dr. Kano is seated front row center with cane. Photo from All-Japan Seibukan Martial Arts and Ways Association.

1

HISTORICAL BACKGROUND

Modern judo is commonly called a sport, a martial art, a way of spiritual harmony, a system of physical education, and a recreational activity. To some extent all of these definitions are appropriate. *Judoka* completely dedicated to the art consider it a way of life; but a full appreciation of the true nature of judo is yet to be attained by its nine million or so exponents. This is because personal interests have narrowed the scope of judo; many of its important cultural aspects have been played down in favor of a few specialized ones.[1]

In order to see judo in its fullest light, it is necessary to look at the origin of *kodokan* judo and its place in the history of Japanese culture.

HISTORICAL ROOTS

The *bakumatsu*, or the "end of the *bakufu* (military government)" was the period of final decay of the Japanese feudal military regime, established by Tokugawa Ieyasu in 1603 and maintained until the late nineteenth century. The *bakumatsu* was caused by the changing domestic and international conditions under which the *shogun* (military leader) could no longer keep the nation effectively segregated from the outside world.

The growing unrest caused many *daimyos* (rich, powerful territory leaders) to convince the *shogun* to return authority of the country to the emperor. This brought about a period called the Meiji Restoration, when the hollow structure of the shogun's *bakufu* crumbled and the Meiji emperor assumed control in 1868.

The so-called "architects" of the restoration proposed a little national cleanup. Their intention was to sweep away more than 700 years of imperial impotence, during which Japan had been ruled by a succession of powerful families, including the Tokugawas.

It should be noted, however, that the Tokugawas did one thing no others in Japanese history had done to date: unite Japan under one leader. The Tokugawa era was a time of total peace and cultivation for the culture of Japan and the traditions of classical *budo* (martial ways). The arts that were once tools of war for the samurai became methods of inner cultivation and self-improvement. In a way, they had to adapt to peaceful times or face extinction. Zen became intricately woven into the fabric of *budo*, making martial arts true ways of *art*, adding a new dimension to *budo*.

Now, however, the Meiji government had to take drastic measures to reconstruct Japan. The progressives saw the need to do away with many feudal institutions, especially those that favored hereditary right over individual merit, as well as arts that were typical trademarks of the Tokugawa era; namely, classical *budo*. A conservative movement favored returning the government to pre-Tokugawa ethics. The clash of the conservatives and the progressives resulted in a convulsive course of politics that was punctuated by actual combat.[2]

There was, however, agreement among Meiji leaders on their fundamental aim: to win the respect of Western nations and thereby redeem their nation from the gross humiliation that they felt it had suffered from the forcible opening of the country to the West.

The Charter Oath, a declaration made in the name of the emperor in 1868, became the platform of the Meiji government. The last of its five articles is significant: "Knowledge shall be sought throughout the world so as to strengthen the foundations of imperial rule." This article was interpreted broadly to mean that, above all, Japan was to be made *fukoku-kyohei*, "a prosperous nation with strong dedication to the government."[3]

Along with this idea came an almost nationwide dislike for the *budo* of the Tokugawa era. Tokugawa *budo* were personal and spiritual; they were for the good of the self, not for the good of the government. Therefore, many feudal arts, such as *jujutsu*, were unofficially banned. The government did not in essence tell Japanese citizens not to practice them, but in order to adapt to *fukoku-kyohei*, they just did not practice them. *Jujutsu* literally fell into disuse. The top *jujutsu* men of the age were giving strong-man exhibitions in the street in order to survive financially. What was once the glory of the samurai was now looked down on.

In order for *budo* to pass into the Meiji Restoration, it had to become a tool to make one a better person for the good of all. In many cases *budo* reverted to *bu-jutsu* (warlike techniques rather than self-cultivation methods), or else entered into the realm of physical education and sport. Sport was for the good of all as well as for the good of oneself; in this light *budo* were accepted by the people, for the good of the people.

Thus the term *sport* meant more than it does today in America. Sport was a complete physical education; it was not just a game. Techniques for killing and defending were still included in the training, but now the emphasis was on using them in a holistic manner.

It is to the credit of one Dr. Jigoro Kano that *jujutsu* survived the Meiji Restoration. He took his beloved *jujutsu* and altered it to adapt to the times. He called his new methodology *judo*.

FROM JUJUTSU TO JUDO

Jujutsu, or the "yielding art," has been known by a dozen different names: *yawara, taijutsu, wajutsu, torite, kogusoku, kempo, hakuda, kumiuchi, shubaku, koshinomawari*, etc.[4] Each type of *jujutsu* has its own system, with many styles to each system. Generally, *jujutsu*'s aim was to develop skill in attack and defense with or without weapons, against an opponent with or without weapons.

The origin of *jujutsu* is vague at best, and what little we do know is more legend than truth. However, the *takenouchi-ryu* (founded by Takenouchi Hisamori) is considered the core *jujutsu* form, having been organized in 1532.

Jujutsu's golden age extended from the late seventeenth century to the mid-nineteenth century. The *jujutsu* systems that were the most popular (there were 725 recorded systems) were *takenouchi-ryu, jikishin-ryu, kyushin-ryu, yoshin-ryu, mirua-ryu, sekiguchi-ryu, kito-ryu*, and *tenshin-shinyo-ryu*; the last two were instrumental in judo's development.

There are many reasons that the samurai turned to *jujutsu* rather than to his main weapon, the sword:

1. The samurai always wore two swords (until the custom was abolished in 1871). When in the presence of high personages, however, the samurai was without his swords. But he still needed to be prepared for battle at all times, so an empty-hand system was needed. Thus *jujutsu* was created. (It should be noted, however, that many styles of *jujutsu* call for training in weapons such as the *jo*, or short staff, and sword.)

2. To make him a better fighter, the samurai needed to learn the special methods of *atemi*, or striking, punching, and kicking. These were an essential part of *jujutsu*.

3. Up until the Meiji Restoration, common people were not allowed to be armed. Therefore, the common people latched on to *jujutsu* as a way of survival.

Again, the new era made the old *jujutsus* relics of the past. But the war of the progressives and the conservatives brought *jujutsu* to the surface again. Its merits were reviewed, and the police began to take an interest in it. This is when Dr. Jigoro Kano entered the scene.

Dr. Kano (1860–1938), teacher, professor, educator, sportsman, philosopher, humanitarian, politician, and *shihan* (*budo* master), originated judo in 1882 when he opened the first judo practice hall at the age of 22. He called it the *kodokan*.

Dr. Kano's rational genius as an educator and his personal idealistic philosophy were of great importance in determining the nature of the original *kodokan* judo.[5] Kano the educator sincerely believed that the health and well-being of a nation depends on the nation's energy. Judo was a way to build that energy and give the nation the foundation it needed so badly.

As a boy, Kano was in and out of bed with one sickness after another. Against his doctor's advice, Kano decided to do something to improve his health, so he enrolled in the *tenshin-shinyo-ryu* school of *jujutsu* in 1877. Under the guidance of his *sensei* (teacher), Fukuda Hachinosuke (who was a student of Iso Ma-taemon, the founder of the system), Kano began his long journey to physical well-being. The *tenshin-shinyo-ryu* was a soft system of *jujutsu* (in many ways similar to *aikido*) that, during the Meiji Period, did not stress combat, but instead harmony. However, the *ryu* (system) still had an excellent reputation for producing fine fighters.

The specialty of the *ryu* was its use of *ate-waza* (striking techniques) and *katame-waza* (grappling) along with *tai-sabaki* (twisting and shifting actions) that were used to take an opponent down effortlessly. Kano's injuries were numerous, but still he continued his training.

When his teacher died, Kano joined the *kito-ryu* system of *jujutsu* under the direct supervision of Iikudo Tsunetoshi. Tsunetoshi's brand of *kito-ryu* was much softer than Kano's previous experience with *jujutsu*. Tsunetoshi stressed *ran*, or "freedom of action," and only moderately strenuous workouts. Attention was instead paid to abstract symbolism connected with physical technique. *Kito-ryu* stressed *nage-waza* (throwing techniques) and effective self-defense "tricks."

After many years with the *kito-ryu* Kano began a comprehensive study of other classical *jujutsus*, especially the arts of *sekiguchi-ryu* and *seigo-ryu*. Kano then began the self-appointed task of making *jujutsu* part of national culture. He did this by updating and refining *jujutsu* for modern Japanese society. He accomplished this in 1882 with the founding of *kokokan* judo.

The term *kodokan* indicates a common spirit of cultural endeavor. *Kodokan* breaks down into *ko* (lecture, study, method), *do* (way or path), and *kan* (hall or place). Thus it means "a place to study the *way*."

The *kodokan* became an official Japanese foundation in 1909, and two years later, in 1911, the Kodokan Black Belt Association was organized. In 1921 the Judo Medical Research Society was born.

Dr. Kano's efforts were not limited to judo but extended over many other horizons. Dr. Kano helped many other sports enter the country, and as such he has been referred to as the "Father of Japanese Sports."

In 1935 he was awarded the Asahi Prize for "outstanding contributions in the fields of art, science, sports." Three years later he went to an International Olympic Council meeting in Cairo, where he succeeded in getting Tokyo nominated as a site for the 1940 Olympics.[6]

On his way home from that momentous conference onboard the SS Hikawa Maru, on May 4, 1938, Jigoro Kano died from pneumonia at the age of 78.[7]

Over the years, Kano had stressed that his art not be referred to as merely *judo*, since two centuries earlier the *jikishin-ryu* used the term *judo* to describe its art. This fact made Kano insist on the prefix *kodokan* when referring to his art.[8]

KODOKAN AND THE IDEALS BEHIND IT

For several reasons, Dr. Kano felt it was very important to keep his new art separate from *jujutsu*. He stated why in a lecture he gave to students at the *kodokan* in 1898:

> I am teaching more than a *jutsu*, "art" or "practice." Of course I teach *jutsu*, but it is upon *do*, "way" or "principle," that I wish to lay special stress. Nowadays it is common for people to say *judo* for *jujutsu*. But before I began to teach judo, the term had been adopted only by the *jikishin-ryu*. It was very rarely used among other schools. I purposely chose this rarely used term in order to distinguish my school from the common run of *jujutsu* schools. . . . There are two other reasons why I avoid the term *jujutsu*. One is that *jujutsu* schools often indulge in violent and dangerous techniques in throwing and twisting arms and legs. Seeing these things, many people have come to believe *jujutsu* is harmful. [Note: Judo does use violent striking and twisting techniques, but only in the advanced black-belt ranks.] . . . The second reason was that when I began to teach, *jujutsu* had fallen into disrepute. Some *jujutsu* masters made their living by organizing troupes composed of their followers and putting on exhibition matches to which ad-

mission fees were charged. Others went so far as to stage bouts between professional *sumo* wrestlers and *jujutsu* men. Such degrading practices of prostituting a martial art were repugnant to me, so I avoided the term *jujutsu* and adopted the term *kodokan judo* instead.[9]

The first *kodokan*, established in 1882, had only 12 mats (12 feet by 18 feet), and the students in the first year numbered only nine. Today the *kodokan* has 500 mats (100 feet by 100 feet) in the main hall and several smaller personal practice rooms. The number of active *judoka* the world over has been estimated at six to nine million.

MODERN JUDO AND THE AAU

It is generally believed in judo circles that the "gentle way," the literal English translation for *judo*, first entered the United States in 1902 when Yoshiaki Yamashita entered the country on the request of Graham Hill, director of the Northern Railroad. One of Yamashita's most prestigious students was President Theodore Roosevelt. Yamashita's wife also taught judo on a limited basis. Her most famous student was Mrs. Wadsworth. The Yamashitas returned to their homeland in 1909.

Next, in 1903, came Tomita Sensei. Tomita had made an impressive name for himself in Japan by besting a police *jujutsuka* (practitioner). In fact, this match did much to establish judo in Japan not only as a sport but as an effective means of combat as well.

After Yamashita and Tomita, many *judoka* arrived on the shores of the United States, some for brief visits, others for permanent residence. One of the most prestigious visitors was Dr. Kano himself, who in 1932 gave special seminars. As a result, four organizations, which in time became recognized bodies of the *kodokan*, were born.

Currently there are some 23 judo associations working within the framework of the United States Judo Association; there are also numerous associations working within the rival organization, the United States Judo

Federation.[10] Each association has some 20,000 members. In addition, there are two organizations representing judo as a cultural activity and method of combat. These are the Dai-Nippon Seibu-kan Budol Bugei-Kai (its American branch is the Seibukan Association of America), with some 9,000 judo members, and the prestigious American Society of Classical Judoka (ASCJ), with some 10,000 members. The ASCJ is an organization that one is asked to join; one does not independently seek membership. Its objective is to establish judo as more than just a sport, but as an actual art form and method of movement meditation

The Olympics first recognized judo in 1964, when Japan hosted the games. Although it was not part of the 1968 games, judo is now an official Olympic sport.

In the Olympics, as well as in the majority of U.S. tournaments, *judoka* compete by weight classifications (see Appendix III for sport rules and official weight divisions). At times, however, there are *rank* tournaments, in which individuals of the same rank fight regardless of weight. In such tournaments proof must be presented to verify one's rank. Naturally, rank is not *usually* recognized if you happen to be a member of an organization other than the one that is sponsoring the event. But times are changing, and one day we may actually see each organization recognizing the other.

To help bring about better world understanding toward differing judo associations, an international body, called the International Judo Federation, was formed in 1952. The aims and purpose of the organization are:

1. to promote cordial and friendly relations among its association members and to coordinate and supervise judo activities in all countries of the world;
2. to protect the interests of judo throughout the world;
3. to organize and conduct the World Judo Championships and judo competitions in the International Olympic Games Program, in conjunction with regional unions;
4. to organize the judo movement throughout the world on an international basis and to promote the spread and development of the spirit and techniques of judo;
5. to establish technical standards;
6. to keep the traditions of judo alive through the *kata* (forms).

2
THEORY

The art of judo is based on the concept of *ju*, or "gentleness," a concept that was used by earlier exponents of many classical *bujutsu* and *budo*. There were many interpretations of *ju*, however, and Dr. Kano thought that many of them were outright misinterpretations of the principle.

These errors, if applied to judo, distort its theory, making it unrealistic and inappropriate for practical implementation. When the principle of *ju* is not fully understood, there will be obvious conflicts between theory and practice.

For our purposes, *ju* can be translated as "giving way." Let us say that the strength of a man standing in front of me is ten units, whereas my lesser strength is represented by seven units. If he pushes me with all his force, I will certainly be pushed back or thrown down, even if I use all my strength against him (ten units are greater than seven). But if, instead of opposing him, I were to give way to his strength by withdrawing my body just as much as he had pushed, taking care at the same time to keep my balance, then he would naturally lean forward and thus lose his balance.

Thus the term *ju yoku go o sei suru* ("softness controls hardness; weakness controls strength") was used by Dr. Kano to explain *ju*. Kano took the concept from the Taoist book, *Tao Te Ching* by Lao-tzu (founder of Taoism). Lao-tzu said, "Reversing is the movement of the Tao." Kano used this quote to form the basis of his own idea that "the most yielding things in the world will master those that do not yield."

That which yields is not necessarily weak or soft in a quantitative sense, though its act of yielding may be so in a relative sense, and it only is temporarily softer or weaker than that which opposes it by being unyielding.

Some martial arts historians actually believe that the concept of *ju yoku go o sei suru*, as Kano had come to understand it, was a part of the *kito-ryu jujutsu* he studied. *Kito-ryu* is very much involved with yin/yang, the Chinese concept of opposites (negative/positive) underlying all universal existence. In fact, the term *kito* comes from the concept of opposition. *Ki* means "to rise," which can be related to *yang*; *to* means "to fall," which can be related to *yin*. In essence, the concept, as applied by the *kito-ryu*, meant that if someone comes at you with strength (*yang*), you should not resist but instead yield (*yin*) to overcome him.

However, it seems that the true source of Kano's inspiration may have come instead from his study of *tenshin-shinyo-ryu*, where the art of yielding has been compared (and called identical) to arts such as modern-day *aikido*.

Tenshin-shinyo-ryu's interpretation identifies *ju* as a submissive quality of the body that subordinates it to the mind—a principle of flexibility of mind in meeting and rapidly adapting oneself to sudden emergencies. This concept in *tenjin-shinyo-ryu* is not called *ju*, however, but rather *karada o shite seishin ni jujun narashimeru jutsu*, or "the art of making the body obedient to the mind."

In many ways this concept is very much similar to the Zen Buddhist concept of *mushin-no-shin*, or "mind of no mind." This concept of *mushin* was the secret of many *ken-jutsu* (sword arts) schools. In fact, those samurai who could apply the principle were nearly undefeatable.

The principle of *ju* as applied to the mechanical execution of judo techniques was found in the expression *kureba mukae, sareba okuru,* which means "when the opponent comes, welcome him; when he goes, send him on his way." It is also sometimes more simply understood as "maximum efficiency with minimum effort."

Dr. Kano explained this:

> The principle of maximum efficiency is fundamental in understanding judo. But it is also something more. The idea is to put him in more than an awkward position. One must take advantage while one is superior in position, using the least amount of effort to take him down. The idea is using his strength against himself, so as to keep my strength in reserve. If I had greater strength than my opponent, I could, of course, push him without him being able to stop me. But even if I wished to, and had the power to do so, it would still be better for me first to give

way, because in doing so, I should have greatly saved my energy and exhausted my opponent's.

> This is one simple instance of how, by giving way, an opponent may be defeated. Such is the principle of *ju*.[1]

THE THREE CULTURE PRINCIPLES

There is a belief among *judoka* that their art is superior to all others in hand-to-hand combat. Many will hear this and say, "Oh, not another one," for indeed each and every style of martial art and each martial artist believes his the best. Kano himself called his art formally *dai Nippon den kodokan judo*, or "best judo in all Japan." This prestigious, if not boastful, expression is on all diplomas of black-belt rank issued by the *kodokan* and used the world over. Naturally, it is impossible to prove or disprove such a statement since one cannot judge an art by the art itself but by its practitioners.

In his extensive study of *jujutsu*, Kano found the expression *shin-shin no chikara a moto no yuko ni shi o suru*, or "whatever the object, the best way of attaining it shall be the best use of energy directed to that purpose or aim." This was later, in 1923, termed *seiryoku zen'yo*, or "the best use of energy."[2]

But Kano had higher goals for his judo when he established the *kodokan*. He broke the goals of judo into two values: *kyogi* (narrow goals) and *kogi* (higher goals).

Kyogi was broken down into (1) acquiring a sound body (*rentai-ho*) and (2) developing expert contest skills (*shobu-ho*). These were judo in the narrow sense because all they did was stress techniques. *Kyogi* should be augmented by *kogi*, which is made up of mental cultivation (*sushin-ho*). *Rentai-ho*, *shobu-ho*, and *sushin-ho* form the three culture principles of Kano.

JUDO ETIQUETTE—REISHIKI

One of the most important fundamentals a beginner of judo learns is *reishiki*, or etiquette. The bow (*rei*) is an outward sign of *reishiki* and an important cultural extension of judo training.

In Japanese, reishiki is literally translated as "salutation or thanks." In Japan of old, reishiki was not a sign of wealth or social standing or of effete prissiness but of the degree to which a person related to others around him. Simply put, reishiki was a mark of one's cultural sensitivity.[3]

To the samurai, manners were not a series of minor measures undertaken to make life more pleasant for others; they were an elaborate system of deportment that made his world a safer and more comfortable place. For instance, since the floors of many homes were covered with thin, fragile rice mats (tatami), footgear was taken off before entering the house to protect another's financial investment. Another example: During the course of Japanese history the roads and highways were infested with bandits and other human parasites. Thus men fell into the habit of walking a couple of steps ahead of their elders or their wives as a protective measure.

Today's judoka does not have to contend with nearly as many details of reishiki as did his predecessors in bujutsu. In the old days, from the moment they stepped into the dojo (practice hall/school), martial artists had to be sure always to face and leave the dojo's shrine leading with the correct foot, to position their skirts (hakama) properly when they sat down, and even to carry their practice weapons in an acceptable fashion. Today's judoka is expected merely to bow at the right times and to seat himself in the right way in the dojo. Yet even these basic manners aren't necessary to learning how to throw. So why adhere to them?

The reasons for reishiki are twofold.[4] First, a basic philosophy of judo is that the way for its practitioners to live honestly, respectfully, and free from the distractions of our busy world is to immerse themselves regularly in an activity that suspends conscious thought. From this perspective, then, how we do something is at least as important as what we're doing. It is through the intricate reishiki that the judoka achieves a state of tranquility that is very practical in and out of the dojo.

Second, apart from the philosophical foundation for reishiki, manners are important to

the judoka because they make him more capable of defending himself. Kano always believed that the root of judo's culture was in its etiquette and manners. He meant that the judoka should always be polite in or out of the dojo. But in addition to this, he meant that if a judoka observes reishiki as a matter of course until it is an unconscious part of his daily behavior, in times of emergency he will react just as automatically in meeting an unexpected attack.

As mentioned previously, the outward sign of reishiki used in modern judo is the rei, or bow. The rei can be performed kneeling (zarei) or standing. There are a variety of ways, both new and old, to perform them (see photos). The rei is performed (1) on entering and leaving the dojo, (2) anytime an instructor (sensei) enters the dojo (all stop and rei), (3) when entering or leaving the tatami (mat) area, (4) before and after a class, (5) before and after a practice, (6) before and after randori (sparring), (7) before and after kata (form training).

At the beginning of a class the zarei is done to the teacher (called sensei rei). The instructor turns and bows very low with the class to the American/Japanese flag and/or the dojo. Last, the instructor turns back to the students, and each bows to represent bowing together and to each other (called shisho rei). The head student of the class (usually the student of highest rank, who is in the front row to his teacher's right) will signal the sensei rei, the teacher will signal the dojo rei, and the head student will signal the shisho rei. Also, other reishiki are followed. First, before class begins the head student, representing all other classmates, will say, "Sensei palchi dojo," or "Teacher, begin to teach us." At the end of class, after bowing, the head student will begin a second formality. He will say, "Sensei moa dojo; sensei noa fi gi shoto arigato," which translates roughly as "Teacher close gym; thank you for your knowledge; we will not abuse it."

Naturally, these formalities are only examples of reishiki. Most schools have their own bowing routines and special reishiki. Those mentioned above are the ones endorsed by the American Society of Classical Judoka.

There are three other reishiki worth men-

2-1–2-4. *Zarei* (kneeling bow): In a kneeling position, bow forward from the waist. Be sure that you sit on your heels and that your hands form a triangle inward.

2-1

2-2

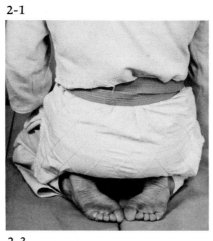

2-3

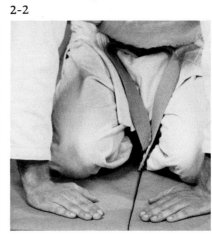

2-4

2-5–2-6. *Rei* (standing bow): Stand relaxed with hands on thighs. Then bend forward from the waist, lowering head.

2-5

2-6

2-7

2-8

2-9

2-10

2-11

2-7. A common alternative to the traditional *rei:* With a lowered head, bow from the waist, with the head up.

2-8. Strength/peace bow: The open left hand signifies peace; the closed right hand signifies power.

2-9. Respect bow: This bow, with the face covered, is the ultimate sign of respect.

2-10. Contemplative bow: Both hands are folded over the chest in prayer position. Head is slightly bowed, with only a minor forward movement from the hips.

2-11. *Obi rei:* Although not a bow in the traditional sense, the *obi rei*—that is, dropping down on one knee while tying the belt—is the traditional method used in *judo kata* (forms).

tioning that are very important to judo: the *gi,* the *dojo,* and hygiene.

The judo *gi,* or uniform, was adapted by Dr. Kano from other schools of *jujutsu* (in fact, the karate *gi* was a lightweight copy of the judo *gi*). The *gi* consists of a jacket, trousers, and a belt (*obi*). The jacket and trousers are an off-white (canvas) color with special knee reinforcements on the pants and extremely tough weaving in the jacket. The jackets can be either single-weave (lightweight) or double-weave (heavyweight/ competition). White is used because it represents a gentleman (*judoka* never wear black *gi,* only a black *hakama,* or skirt, in some formal *kata*).

The belts are graded as follows: white, yellow, orange, green, blue, brown, black, red and white, red, and white. (See Appendix I for a complete history and explanation of the ranking system.) The wearing and tying of the belt are very traditional and are explained in greater detail in the accompanying photos.

The *judoka* must take good care of their *gi,* always keeping them clean and attending to any necessary mending or patching. When carrying them, it is advisable to fold them in the following manner:

1. The jacket and pants are put one over the other.
2. The costume is folded in two.
3. The costume is tied with the belt (*obi*).

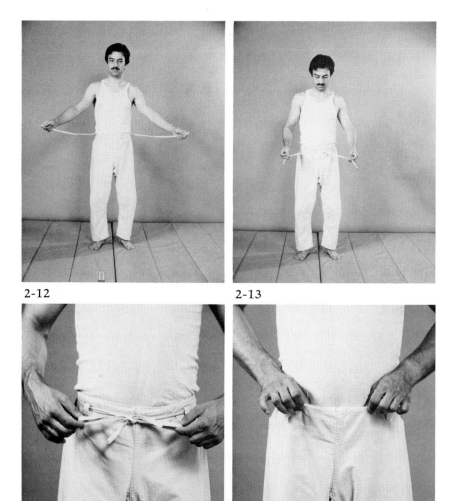

Proper wearing of the *gi:* Put pants on with loops facing forward and strings drawn tightly. Place strings through loops, and tie. Tuck loops into the pants to prevent them from coming untied.

2-12

2-13

2-14

2-15

2-16

2-17

Proper tying of the belt: Place right end of the jacket in first, and then place left end over it. Gather the belt in the center and place it over the navel. Draw belt ends around body and bring to the front. Place the left end of the belt over the right and tuck the right end under the entire belt. Pull until it's snug. Put the left end over the right and draw the left end through the loop and secure a square knot. Photo 2-22 shows the completed knot.

2-18

2-20

2-21

2-22

The *dojo,* or training hall, is more than a place to work out, and *reishiki* stresses several of its other values. First, the *dojo* is a place of culture; one must therefore compose oneself and behave seriously (talking idly or acting noisily are prohibited). Both at the time of practice and during a match, one must apply full energy to the technique. Even in repose, one must maintain good deportment and pay attention to others who are exercising, in order to try to learn some lessons that will be helpful in improving oneself. One must never lean against the wall but must always stand or kneel with back straight. Finally, cooperation should be the ruling spirit (*zanshin*) to keep the *dojo* well arranged, clean, and in order, since it is the house of all who use it.

The last *reishiki* we will discuss is etiquette toward oneself, or, more simply, hygiene. If one wishes to secure the best results from the practice of judo, one must observe moderation in eating (see Appendix II, on diet for judo), drinking, and sleeping. One must also, as a matter of course, refrain from eating and drinking liquids (except small amounts of water under *extremely* hot conditions) during a workout. In order to obtain sound sleep, one must always finish everything to avoid being disturbed. Keeping one's body clean and wearing neat *gi* is necessary not only for health but also out of consideration for others. One should remember to pare one's nails, repair one's *gi,* and make oneself comfortable before beginning exercises. During a workout one should close the mouth and breathe through the nose (except during special breathing exercises).

BALANCE: THE ART OF KEEPING IT AND BREAKING IT

The theory of throwing an opponent off balance is the most important part of practical judo theory. In essence, the theory of balance can be broken down into several categories: (1) *shintai,* (2) *tai-sabaki* (body movement), (3) the use of force, (4) *kuzushi* (breaking balance), (5) *tsukuri* (attack preparation), and (6) *kake* (attack).

Shintai (Advance/Retreat)

Shintai is fundamental to execution of judo techniques, especially throwing (*nage-waza*) techniques. *Shintai* can best be described as "movement" applied either right to left, or advancing/retreating.

In general, whenever you move forward or backward to apply a technique you will place the weight of the body over the lead foot. When in close, the *tsugi-ashi* should be used *(see Diagram 1).*

To master *tsugi-ashi,* you must first master the "follow" method of walking. Most people naturally walk by putting their weight on one foot and advancing the other, then shifting their weight to the advancing foot when it makes solid contact with the ground.

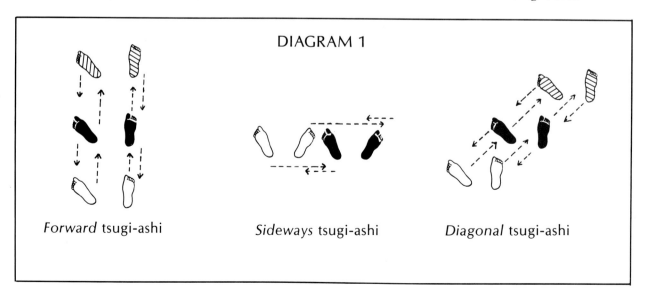

DIAGRAM 1

Forward tsugi-ashi   *Sideways* tsugi-ashi   *Diagonal* tsugi-ashi

In *tsugi-ashi* you must move your legs, hips, and body forward or backward all the time. You must not put one foot forward and leave the other behind, or advance your body and leave the other foot behind.

To master it you must maintain a natural body position, with your weight distributed equally (see "Standing Postures and Holding Techniques" in this chapter), and walk with your hips keeping the weight equal on both feet. This can be applied forward, backward, or to either side *(see Diagram 1)*.

Tai-Sabaki (Movement Control)

One learns through *shintai* to advance and retreat. In *tai-sabaki* we learn to step into a throwing position. There are six points in *tai-sabaki* to keep in mind:[5]

1. *Head Position.* Carry your head so that you visualize it resting on your hips (deep) rather than on your shoulders (shallow).
2. *Eye Awareness.* Fix your gaze on your opponent's chest, shoulders, or top of head (never eye to eye); make your gaze narrow, concentrating only on the matter at hand.
3. *Breath Control.* It is important to keep your breath even during the execution of *tai-sabaki*, breathing deeply with the diaphragm and concentrating on a point two inches below your navel (*hara*).
4. *Center.* When pivoting, make all movements come from the center of your body. Do not use just your hands and feet but rather move from the torso so as to maximize your strength with the least effort.
5. *Hand Movements.* Never allow your hands to be trapped; keep them free and in control at all times.
6. *Grounding.* *Tai-sabaki* is, of course, performed with the feet, but judo carries the concept of foot movement even further with the term *grounding*. When moving, always picture yourself grounded to the mat as if an invisible force is holding you firmly and inextricably rooted in place. You should imagine that this force holding you is firm yet swift so you can rapidly shift your weight.

The basic *tai-sabaki* is illustrated in **Diagram 2**, the two most common being pivot forward and pivot sideways.

The Use of Force

The idea behind force in judo is to get the most effect with the least amount of force. When throwing an opponent off balance, you must apply the correct body shift (either *tsugi-ashi* or *tai-sabaki*). If, however, you don't apply force correctly, the encounter may turn into a brute-force match rather than an execution of skill.

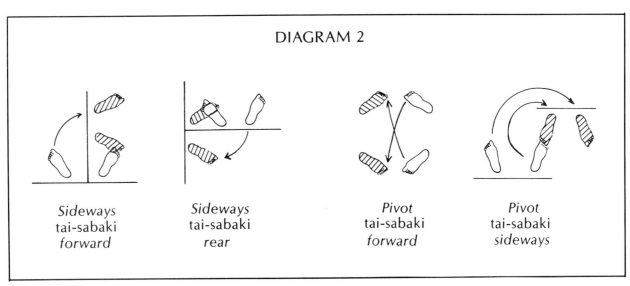

DIAGRAM 2

Sideways tai-sabaki forward

Sideways tai-sabaki rear

Pivot tai-sabaki forward

Pivot tai-sabaki sideways

Use of force is broken down into three points: push when pulled/pull when pushed; push/pull, pull/push; and generation of force.

Push When Pulled/Pull When Pushed

This is fairly self-explanatory. If your opponent is pushing against you and he is stronger than you are, to resist him is futile. But if you use the concepts of centering and grounding and do not resist the push, but instead pull with him, you are applying very little strength to take your opponent down. The same applies in reverse.

The key to making this use of strength work is correct timing and calmness of mind. The trick to downing him easily is to sense the intention of pushing or pulling in your opponent's mind before the action itself actually begins. This will come about through practice and meditation (see Chapter 3).

Push/Pull, Pull/Push

The technique above consisted of going with your opponent's action by not resisting him. This one deals with creating the opportunity by making your opponent commit himself to a motion that you can offset, allowing you to take him down. This is done in three parts:

1. First push your opponent. The natural reaction to being pushed is to resist the push. When he resists the push, pull him in the direction of his resistance and take him down. Again, this requires superior timing and *tai-sabaki*.
2. First pull your opponent. The natural reaction to being pulled is to resist the pull by pulling back. When the opponent commits himself to a pulling action, push with the pull and take the opponent down. The key is to shift smoothly and with flawless timing into the push.
3. Flip the opponent up. When the opponent and you are together at such close quarters that pushing and pulling are both impossible, this method of applying force is effective. You use your entire body to flip your opponent up and force him off balance by raising him from the floor. In this action you use the force of both arms and the spring action of your legs, knees, and hips.

Generation of Force

We have discussed applying force, but at this point we are concerned with applying all of our force at the correct point. You must be able to do this immediately and boldly, but this is impossible if the body is tense and is not centered and grounded. The keys:

1. Never become so preoccupied with off-balancing an opponent that you leave yourself in a bad position to apply force. In other words, push/pull does little good when you have your opponent off balance but you yourself are not in position to do anything.
2. Always remain calm so as to be ready to take advantage of the opportunity with all your power.

Kuzushi (Breaking Balance)

In the uses of force we began a fundamental observation of off-balancing strategy. Now we will look at the way to make the strategy easier to pull off. Getting your opponent into a position at which it will be easy to throw him is the name of the *kuzushi* game. It was Dr. Kano who discovered this principle. He said:

> Sensei Iikudo [*kito-ryu* teacher; see Chapter 1] was over fifty years old at the time, but he was still strong, and I used to work with him often. Although I practiced my technique industriously, I could never vie with him. I think it was about 1885 that I found, while practicing *randori* (free-sparring) with him, that the techniques I tried were extremely effective. Usually it had been he who threw me. Now, instead of being thrown, I was throwing him with increasing regularity. I could do this despite the fact that he was of the *kito-ryu* school and was especially adept at throwing techniques.
>
> This apparently surprised him, and he was

upset over it for quite awhile. What I had done was quite unusual. But it was the result of my study of how to break the posture of the opponent. It is true that I had been studying the problem for some time, together with that of reading the opponent's motion. But it was here that I had first tried to apply the principle of breaking the opponent's posture before the throw. Afterward, at the *kodokan,* I taught this principle as the *happo-no-kuzushi* [breaking the opponent's posture in eight directions; see *Diagram 3*].

In short, the crux of the study was that a human body would lose its balance if it was only pushed backward or pulled forward. A careless standing man, however large or strong, leans backward if pushed from the front or forward if pulled to the front; his posture is broken. . . . Soon after my explaining this to Sensei Iikudo, I was initiated in the mystery of the *kito-ryu jujutsu* and received all books and manuscripts of the school.[6]

Breaking an opponent's posture can be divided into several parts: (1) direction, (2) coordination, and (3) taking advantage of reaction time.

1. *Direction of Breaking.* In which direction should you break an opponent's posture if you are to use maximum efficiency with the least amount of effort? The larger the base, the more stable the body is. Thus, if your opponent stands still, it is best to break his balance forward or backward in the direction of an imaginary perpendicular to the straight line passing through the toes of both feet. If you try to break his posture toward the right or left, the force needed will be much greater because of the greater base; this would not be applying "maximum efficiency with the least amount of effort."

If he is in motion, it is best to push or pull him in the direction of his movement. If you apply force to him in the direction in which he moves, two forces—yours and his—will work on him and cause him to lose his balance. To visualize this more clearly refer to *Diagram 3* and the accompanying photos.

2. *Coordination.* Whenever you initiate the use of force combined with the principles of *kuzushi* you will commit your opponent by off-balancing him. Much of his weight and power will be thrown at you when he is off balance, since as a human being your opponent will instinctively clutch and claw to regain his posture.

As the defender (or attacker, whichever the case may be) you must be ready to coordinate your body and foot movements to take full advantage of his commitment of force and take him to the ground.

It is very important to break your opponent's posture with your *body* and not your hands. There are two reasons for this: First, using the whole body (and centering) in-

---

DIAGRAM 3

The eight points surrounding the feet are the happo-no-kuzushi (eight points of off-balance). These·represent all directions in which an opponent can be off-balanced to correctly apply nage-waza (throwing techniques). They are (1) rear, (2) left rear, (3) left side, (4) left front, (5) front, (6) right front, (7) right side, and (8) right rear.

2-23   2-24

Happo-no kuzushi (direction of throwing). The four major directions for off-balancing are: forward (photo 2-23); backward (photo 2-24); to the right side (photo 2-25); and to the left side (photo 2-26).

2-25   2-26

creases your force manyfold. Second, by using your body you can better adapt and recover from your own actions.

3. *Taking advantage of your opponent's reaction time.* In the two preceding sections on *kuzushi* we have looked first at the direction in which you can break your opponent's posture and second at the coordination of the body to recover from and use your off-balancing actions. Now let us consider ways to make the opponent's reaction time longer and make use of it in a practical manner.

When you attack your opponent time and again, the second or third attacks may enable you to make a decisive action. This happens because the first and second attacks put him in disorder while you place yourself in your throwing position; thus, you have taken advantage of his force and long reaction time. For example, let us say you attack him with an *o-soto-geri* throw (major outside leg sweeping throw). He must push his upper body forward to resist being thrown. At this point the opponent is locked into the idea of returning to a stable position. He doesn't realize how his pushing force sets him up for a *tai-otoshi* (body drop), a throw that throws him because of his forward leaning—on his back.

The second point is that no matter how good you are you must always be ready to escape your opponent's attack. Whatever direction in which you escape, always do so holding firmly to the principle of *ju* (yielding).

The working of this principle will be shown clearly if you dexterously escape from your opponent's attack. He will break his posture by lengthening his reaction time himself, since he attacks you with all his strength. At this moment you are put into a position that is extremely convenient for applying a throw.

The principle of *ju* should be applied only during advancing and retreating. To take advantage of both your opponent's force and his long reaction time, you must move faster and farther than he does. Through this method, if you repeat it consecutively, you will finally throw him off balance. No matter what posture you take in accordance with his motion, you must be able to return to a position of natural posture before he attacks you.[7]

Tsukuri and Kake (Preparation for Attack, Attack)

Although not referred to by these terms, these concepts have been explained in other sections of off-balancing. *Tsukuri* refers to any action used to set up a throw and involves physical as well as mental and emotional preparation. *Kake* refers to the actual execution of a technique.

STANDING POSTURES AND HOLDING TECHNIQUES

The two most basic postures for executing throwing techniques are the *shizentai* or "natural" posture and the *jigotai* or "defensive" posture.

The natural position is adopted by placing your feet shoulder width apart with weight distributed equally on both feet, bending *slightly* with the knees, and keeping the back straight and relaxed. Remember to breathe and concentrate on your center (*tan tien*), the point located two inches below the navel. Also, the use of timing and calmness of mind (see "The Use of Force" in this chapter) are very important in staying stable.

2-27   2-28   2-29

Kuzushi (breaking balance). Basic *kuzushi* is applied to the front (photo 2-27), rear (photo 2-28), and side (photo 2-29). Through correct application of *kuzushi*, the *judoka* weakens an opponent's posture, enabling the *judoka* to apply one of many throws.

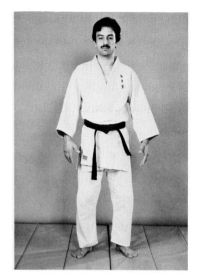

2-30. *Shizentai* (natural posture)

2-31. *Hidari shizentai* (left natural posture)

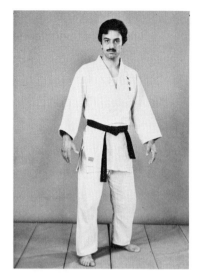

2-32. *Migi shizentai* (right natural posture)

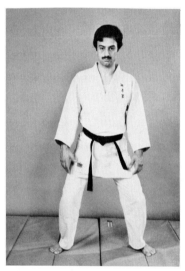

2-33. *Jigotai* (defensive posture)

2-34. *Hidari jigotai* (left defensive posture)

2-35. *Migi jigotai* (right defensive posture)

2-36 Holding grips: Grip A

2-37 Grip B

2-38 Grip C

The natural posture can be performed to either the right or the left by placing the left or right foot forward from the basic posture with the heel of your rear foot turned *slightly* inward (see accompanying photos). The advantages of the *shizentai* posture, either *migi-shizentai* (right natural posture) or *hidari-shizentai* (left natural posture), are (1) the ability to move quickly from posture to posture, (2) the ability to stand in posture for prolonged periods, (3) the lack of fatigue by keeping posture, and (4) the flexibility, which makes it the most effective posture from which to execute throwing techniques.

The defensive posture, or *jigotai*, is adopted by placing your feet farther apart than in the *shizentai* posture, almost as if you were sitting on a horse. Again, be sure to keep your back straight and relaxed, your body centered, and your feet grounded. From the basic *jigotai* stance you can perform *migi-jigotai* (right defensive) or *hidari-jigotai* (left defensive) posture by advancing with either your left or your right foot (see accompanying photos).

The advantage of the *jigotai* posture is its apparent stability in tight situations. However, it is not as versatile and, in the long run, not as stable (because of its lack of flexibility) as the *shizentai* posture. Thus, keep in mind that *shizentai* is the major posture, and *jigotai* is a secondary, or backup, position.

Once the *judoka* has mastered the standing postures he moves on to understanding the subtle complexities of the *kumikata*, or grabbing techniques. There are two concerns in *kumikata*: (1) how to grab the *gi* (uniform), and (2) how to stand when grabbing.

The *gi* can be grabbed in grip A (both hands on the lapel), grip B (both hands on the sleeves) or grip C (one hand on the lapel and the other on the sleeve). Grip C is the grip used most often in competitive and form judo.

Grabbing an opponent can be done in either a *shizentai* or *jigotai* posture.

Standing in *Shizentai*

We will explain the right natural position.

The left natural position will be the exact opposite. Face your opponent in a right natural position, taking his left lapel in your right hand and his right sleeve in your left hand. A note on grabbing the *gi*: whatever part you grab, remember to do so using your little finger and ring finger together. If you are grabbing the jacket, thrust your little finger and ring finger in and then catch the material and pull. At the same time, add your index finger and relax your thumb. Let your thumb rest lightly on the cloth of his jacket, because if you tense your thumb you will spoil the movement of your feet.[8]

Standing in *Jigotai*

Jigotai can be performed in one of two ways: (1) classical, which is nearly identical to the *shizentai* explanation above, except the feet are in a horse-type *jigotai* posture; (2) modern, in which you assume a right *jigotai* posture, place your right hand under your opponent's left arm, and put the tips of your fingers and the palm of your hand on his back (over the shoulder blade). Do not grab the *gi*. With your left hand, grasp the outer upper part of the left sleeve and hold his right arm with your left armpit. It is important that you keep the chin pulled in. Keep your armpits close to your body (the left *jigotai* is the opposite of right).

Rules for *Kumikata*

1. Always *stand natural* to your opponent; that is, if your opponent assumes a right position, you follow suit; if he chooses a left posture, you do the same.
2. Do not tense your upper body, especially your arms. Compare it to water running through a hose. If the hose is bent, the water stops flowing. So too, if your arms are tense, the energy of your body stops flowing.
3. Always change your posture with your opponent as you apply a wide variety of techniques. Never stick to one posture.

3
HOLISTIC CONDITIONING

When I was preparing for the National East Coast Judo Championships, an AAU event, in 1974, I found that the key ingredient to my training was conditioning of both body and spirit.

The body conditioning was fairly standard as far as judo is concerned, but my spiritual and mental conditioning was accomplished through my study of yoga, a physical exercise system that is used to integrate mind, body, and spirit through *asanas*, or body postures.

I learned the value of yoga training in 1970, when I spent the first of three summers at Eisho-ji, a Zen community in Corning, New York. When I finished my training my competitive ability in judo and karate was increased tenfold. In addition, I had acquired a calmness of mind that was useful in and out of the *dojo*. When I finished my meditative study at Eisho-ji in 1972 I entered numerous judo competitions and won each one in open weight divisions (I weigh 140 pounds). It is my feeling that it was my "integration" that led to my victories, not any superior technique I used.

INTEGRATION
The current trend in judo training would have you believe that almost anything—increased strength, increased stamina, etc.—can be accomplished through some form of weight training.

Competitive skill has, in many cases, been replaced by sheer competitive strength—the stronger you are, the better you can defeat your opponent (what happened to technique?). Other factors that are sometimes added to this are proper diet, strong conditioning, positive mental attitude, etc.

While such activities are indeed extremely beneficial, one very important element has consistently been omitted. The missing dimension in judo training has nothing to do with what we normally think of as competitive conditioning. What I am talking about is integration of mind, body, and spirit, accomplished through yoga *asanas* (postures), yoga *pranayama* (breathing), and meditation.

To begin with, the physical body of a *judoka* is only one-quarter of the whole person. Each person also has a mental body (thoughts and cognitive mind), an emotional body (feelings and desires), and an etheric body (your memory, containing layers of subconscious and superconscious mind as well as the blueprint for life) to train for optimum performance in any aspect of judo—especially competition.

These three other bodies fulfill a very important role in any judo training program. They support the physical body and give it that extra determination to work those muscles, even when—and *especially* when—you feel that "burn" that lets you know you are making progress.

As anyone familiar with judo (or physical fitness in general) can testify, workouts are grueling and painful (more so in judo than in most other sports), and they exact a heavy toll on the body. Except for a possible *endorphin*-induced high, there is little immediate gratification (*endorphins* are chemicals the body produces during periods of *intense* exertion that mimic the effects of opium on the brain).

Another phenomenon known in judo (and other sports) is the "wall." This is the point at which the body has used up all its available glycogen and has no more energy to give to the muscles. Sometimes drinking sugar water or taking teaspoons of honey (the better of the two) can combat this problem. Most people will get exhausted, however, long before the *wall* is reached.

The point I am making is that most people could work out intensively for many hours but stop prematurely because they think or feel that they can't do it. This is seen especially in competition, when a *judoka* stops trying. If these individuals could get their mental and emotional bodies working with their physical body, they would excel.

Any gratification gained from a solid judo program comes after the fact. Whether it's drinking a glass of juice and taking a cool shower after a heavy workout or long-term muscular gain, the joy of a workout is not the workout itself.

Consequently, unless you are one who enjoys pain, other factors must drive you to put your body through the rigors of judo. These could be your *memories* of how good you felt the last time you exercised, your *mental* determination to excel, or your desire to attain *emotional* control that comes with true mastery of judo.

True mastery of judo is achieved through integration, especially that of the emotional body with the physical body.

Judo requires a great deal of memory, as do most martial arts and ways, in addition to emotional control. Not only must the *judoka* have a strong, flexible body; he must also remember with intimate detail the complexity of each movement, the exact angle for proper execution, etc.

Once memorized in each brain cell, these responses must then become automated—like a bioelectric reaction invoked and executed faster than the mind can think.

As far as mental attitude is concerned, one should be calm as well as "psyched up" for a game. No matter how skilled your opponent or what rank he may be, you must have the determination to give it all you have and to win.

What does this have to do with yoga? Yoga is the *key* element in integrating the mind, body, and spirit, something judo alone cannot do. Therefore, true competitive ability comes with a strong conditioning program in yoga and more conventional exercises. We will look at both.

YOGA POSTURES

Yoga postures (*asanas*) are not exercises in the sense of practice done with quick movements and a measure of strain involved. *Asana* means posture, or a position that grants steadiness and comfort.

Yoga *asanas* will grant *judoka* several things:

1. integration, as mentioned earlier;
2. a sound physical body, which can cure itself of many ailments and injuries;
3. greater mental alertness; and
4. improved flexibility.

It is important to point out, however, that yoga is *not*, nor was it ever intended to be, a system of flexibility exercises. Anyone who approaches yoga with this idea will eventually be harmed physically and emotionally.

The yoga *asanas* affect the body's endocrine system, making the body produce, or stop producing, various hormones. If you do not follow the directions *exactly* for each posture, harm can be the direct result. The key to attaining the benefits of yoga with this book are to *read* the explanations of each posture and *follow them.*

Points of Interest on Yoga

Time

Yoga should be done directly before each workout for about 30–45 minutes. Many benefits result from this: a soft warmup before more conventional exercises; integration before workout; and calmness before training.

If you are not working out on a particular day but still want to do yoga, it should be done in the morning on awakening or in the evening before sleeping. If you are stiff in the morning, a brisk walk will make you more flexible. Beginners find themselves better "psyched" for yoga, both physically and mentally, in the evenings.

Cleanliness and Food

Before starting to practice postures, the bladder should be empty and the bowels evacuated. Headstand poses will help one evacuate the bowels before attempting more advanced postures.

Place

If you are not doing yoga in the *dojo*, but instead at home, pick a quiet place that is well ventilated. Always use the same place at home in order to relate the location with yoga. When you are in the *dojo*, do yoga on the mats; at home, do yoga on a rug or a folded blanket on a flat surface.

Breathing

Breathing should be done through the nostrils and not the mouth. Breathe with the diaphragm about six times a minute with the the tongue on the roof of the mouth. Breathing should be even. Do not hold your breath during any point of a posture.

Special Provisions for Women

- Avoid doing yoga postures during peak times of menstruation, except if flow is lower than normal. In any case, never do headstand postures during a menstrual period.
- During early pregnancy, light judo training is OK; however, during the later months judo is impossible. Yoga can still be done with light movement right to the moment of delivery, and the *pranayama* breathing exercises can be done right through labor and beyond.
- After delivery no postures can be done for four weeks. Thereafter, begin mild training until you have regained your full strength and can begin judo training again. Doing yoga during these times will help a female *judoka* keep herself in good condition and help her get back to active judo play sooner.

Asana 1: Headstand (*Sirshana*)

Technique

Kneel, lock the fingers, and create an angle with the floor with your forearms by placing them on the floor in front of you. Place the crown of the head on the floor, close to the locked fingers, so the fingers and forearms can support the head. Slowly lift the trunk and bring it perpendicular to the ground by raising the knees and bringing the toes close to the head (*see photo 3-1*). When the trunk is raised you will feel the toes and legs can be lifted off the ground with no jumping or jerking.

After performing the technique for a couple of sessions, slowly lift the toes and fold the legs so that the heels come close to the buttocks, with the soles facing up. Gently lift the thighs, bringing them to a vertical position (*see photo 3-2*). Keep the spine erect. When

3-1   3-2   3-3

3-4   3-5   3-6

coming down, perform the reverse of what has been mentioned.

Variation 1 (Salamba Sirshana)

This is the same as the standard yogic headstand except the hands form a tripod support position *(see photo 3-3)* and the erect body is supported by the action of the hands and head *(see photo 3-4)*. Note: This headstand is easier for a beginner and can be substituted in the beginning stages for the *sirshana* posture.

Variation 2 (Mukta Hasta Sirshana)

A very difficult headstand, this one should

be done only by advanced students *(see photo 3-5)*.

Variation 3

A more advanced version of Variation 2, this position places extreme stress on the neck and back since the only support is provided by the head and neck. The hands merely help keep your balance *(see photo 3-6)*. This is an extremely difficult headstand that should be done only when you master all others.

Benefits

Turning the body upside down is extremely

healthful. Blood flow is increased in the upper half of the body, aiding the brain and respiratory organs. This posture also affects the pineal, pituitary, thyroid, and parathyroid glands. It is especially helpful in relieving headaches and nervous tension. Before any tournament, I would always assume a headstand for 20 minutes or so to aid concentration and relaxation.

Time

At the beginning, hold this posture for only a few seconds so the neck and back muscles will develop the proper strength. After about the first month, hold the posture for 10 minutes. Advanced *judoka* may hold it for 25–30 minutes.

Asana 2: Scorpion Pose (*Pincha Mayurasana*)

Technique

It is best for the beginner to learn the scorpion position by first assuming a standard yogic headstand. When your balance feels secure and you are centered in a straight line, turn your forearms and hands so they face the floor. Using your arms for support, lift yourself up, relying on balance and shoulder/arm strength. Arch the body slightly backward for better balance (*see photo 3-7*).

Variation

After assuming the standard scorpion position, arch your back farther forward, bring one leg down, and bend the other inward (*see photo 3-8*).

Benefits

This posture develops the muscles of the shoulders and back. It tones the spine and stretches the abdominal muscles.

Time

See Asana 1.

Asana 3: Shoulder Stand (*Sarvangasana*)

Technique

Lie flat on your back, placing your hands alongside the body. Raise the legs to a 90-degree angle with the floor. Then raise the trunk of the body to a vertical position as well, until the chin presses against the chest. As you raise the trunk, simultaneously raise the forearms to support the back. The entire body is arched, with knees near the forehead (*see photo 3-9*). Raise the legs so the entire body, from neck to toes, is as straight as possible. To come down, return the knees to the head, return the arms to your sides, lower the back to the ground, and then lower the legs to the ground (*see photo 3-10*).

3-7 3-8 3-9 3-10

Benefits

This posture promotes tremendous flexibility in the neck. It also will do wonders for back disorders and shoulder ailments. For those *judoka* who suffer from asthma and hernia, this posture is of specific interest. By tipping the body upside-down and extending and erecting the chest cavity, this *asana* expands the breathing cavity in the chest area, allowing the body to take in more oxygen. Also, being tipped upside down allows the mucus a chance to break up, adding to freer breath. Hernia sufferers will find that by tipping the body in this fashion the hernia will actually disappear for a short time, allowing blood to the herniated area to promote healing. Many research studies are under way at this time on the therapeutic effects of being upside down.

Caution: (1) Keep the mouth closed. If saliva collects, *do not* swallow it. (2) If you feel like coughing, sneezing, etc., come down from this position first. (3) Do not perform this posture if you have a fever.

Time

Beginners should hold this for one minute. Advanced students can hold it for up to five minutes.

Asana 4: The Plow (*Halasana*)

Technique

This posture is usually done as an extension of the shoulder stand, but it can be done from a prone position as well. The idea is to perform the posture without bending the knees, keeping the fingertips and/or palm on the ground *(see photo 3-11)*.

Note: Hold your breath in this posture when you are bringing the legs over the head and until the feet are on the floor; then continue to deep-breathe normally.

Variation

Instead of leaving the arms in back, wrap the arms behind the head *(see photo 3-12)*.

Variation 2

To stretch the body further, bring the knees to the floor behind your head *(see photo 3-13)*.

Benefits

This posture is excellent for making the spine flexible. Patanjali, the founder of *hatha* (physical) yoga, said, "You are as young as your spine is flexible." This posture is good for curing indigestion.

Time

Beginners should hold this for 3–10 seconds, but it can be held safely for five minutes.

Asana 5: Locust Pose (*Salabhasana*)

Technique

Lie facedown with hands along your sides or crossed under the abdomen. Rest the chin on the floor (or, as some prefer, turn the head and rest the face on the floor). Inhale and raise the right leg, keeping the leg as straight as possible. Bring the leg up as far as it will go comfortably and hold *(see photo 3-14)*. Lower. Repeat with the left leg.

Variation

Use the same technique as above, but this time lift both legs at the same time *(see photo 3-15)*.

Benefits

This is excellent for building lower abdominal and back muscles—a must for throwing techniques such as *harai-goshi* (sweeping hip throw).

Time

Hold this as long as is comfortable, not exceeding three minutes.

3-11   3-12   3-13

3-14   3-15

3-16   3-17

Asana 6: The Cobra (*Bhujangasana*)

Technique

Lie on the floor facedown, resting the entire body *(see photo 3-16)*. Arch the body upward, keeping the lower abdominal region on the floor *(see photo 3-17)*.

Benefits

A strong, elastic spine and elastic but strong upper abdominal muscles can be developed with this posture.

Time

Up to three times is beneficial; beyond that point is unnecessary. However, since this pose expands the chest cavity, asthmatics can stay in this position for up to ten minutes to aid in breathing.

Asana 7: Stretching Peacock Pose (*Mayurasana*)

Technique

Kneel on all fours, with hands about

shoulder width apart. Bend forward, invert the palms (fingers pointing toward feet), and place them on the floor. Lift the body off the floor, balancing with the arms. Feet can be raised to three levels: level (parallel to floor), middle, and high (vertical) position. The middle position is pictured (see photo 3-18).

Variation

Technique is the same as above, but keep the forearms together and balance.

Benefits

This posture tones the abdominal region. Due to pressure on the elbows, the posture is good for developing arm strength and wrist flexibility.

Time

Hold for one minute.

Asana 8: Fish Pose (Matsyasana)

Technique

Sit in a lotus posture (see "Asana 33: Meditative Poses") and lie flat on your back with legs on the floor. Lift your back with your head and form an arch (see photo 3-19).

Benefits

This posture expands the chest cavity, aiding in the judoka's quest for a fuller breath. The posture also stretches the back and neck.

Asana 9: Head-to-Knee Pose (Jaschimothanasana)

Technique

Lie flat on your back, stretching the arms over the head and alongside you on the floor, locking the thumbs. The upper arms should almost touch the ears. Stiffen the entire body, holding your breath, and slowly raise the arms, head, and chest simultaneously,

assuming a sitting position with arms stretching over the head. Make sure the arms do not descend and the legs do not jerk upward as you rise. Then, slowly bend forward, exhaling and holding onto the big toe with the index finger and thumb of both hands. Sustain the pose, breathing normally. Little by little, bring the face down to the knee until it touches the knee or (advanced) the floor (see photo 3-20).

Benefits

This is an excellent stretching pose, and it tones nearly every muscle in the body. The posture also improves circulation in the thighs.
Caution: Do not stretch in the traditional sense. If you feel tightness or pain, stop there and hold the posture in this position. Yoga is not stretching, so don't turn it into a stretching workout.

Time

Hold for one minute.

Asana 10: Double Head-to-Knee Pose (Janusirshasana)

Technique

This is the same as head-to-knee pose, except you use both legs (see photo 3-21)

Variation

Instead of locking the big toe with the index finger and thumb, reach over the foot and grasp the heel (see photo 3-22). This is a very advanced version of the standard double head-to-knee pose.

Benefits

See Asana 9.
Caution: See Asana 9.

Time

See Asana 9.

3-18

3-19

3-20

3-21

3-22

3-23

Asana 11: Backlift Position (*Supta Vajtasana*)

Technique

Lie on the floor with hands at your sides and relax completely. Bring your feet to your hands, grasp the ankles, and inhale. Raise your back, keeping your head on the floor, and exhale *(see photo 3-23)*. Continue breathing normally in this position.

Benefits

Strong buttock muscles and flexibility in the shoulders are the benefits of this posture.

Time

Hold for as long as is comfortable.

Asana 12: Mountain Bending Posture (*Parvatasana*)

Technique

Assume a lotus posture (see "Asana 33: Meditative Poses") and interlace the fingers behind your back. Bend forward and place either your forehead or the side of your face on the floor *(see photo 3-24).*

Benefits

This pose is believed to strengthen and turn on the senses. A more practical benefit is superior flexibility in mid-back and upper thighs.

Time

Hold for one minute maximum.

Asana 13: Child Pose (*Virasana*)

Technique

This is a very simple pose, used mostly for relaxation. Assume a kneeling meditative pose (see "Asana 33: Meditative Poses") and lower the head to the floor, holding on to the heels or interlacing fingers behind soles of the feet *(see photo 3-25).*

Benefits

In addition to relaxation, the child pose is believed to strengthen the knees.

Time

Hold for as long as desired.

Asana 14: Lying-Down Extension Pose (*Supta Padangusthasana*)

Technique

Relax, lying on your back, inhaling and exhaling for a few counts. Bring one knee up to the chest and hold it tightly yet comfort-ably *(see photo 3-26).* Holding the ball of the foot, extend the leg fully, bringing it down to the head *(see photo 3-27).* Repeat with the other leg.

Benefits

A general strengthening of the leg socket as well as increased flexibility of the upper thigh can result from this *asana.*

Time

Hold for only a few seconds.

Asana 14: Lying-Down Double Extension Pose (*Urdhva Mukha Paschimottanasana*)

Technique

Lie down on your back and slowly, *without tension,* bring the knees to the chest, grasping and holding them to the chest firmly but without pain or tension *(see photo 3-28).* Grasp the balls of the feet, extend the legs, and bring the knees to the head *(see photo 3-29).*

Benefits

This pose will improve balance and poise since it seems to affect the body's sense of balance in the inner ear. The pose is also useful for relieving severe backaches.

Asana 15: Bow and Arrow Pose (*Akarna Dhanurasana*)

Technique

Grasp the ball of both feet (or in some methods the big toe with index finger and thumb) and draw one foot back to your ear as if drawing a bow with an arrow *(see photo 3-30).* Release the arrow by straightening the leg held near the ear *(see photo 3-31).*

Benefits

This pose will promote excellent flexibility in the legs. Also, the lower portion of the spine is exercised.

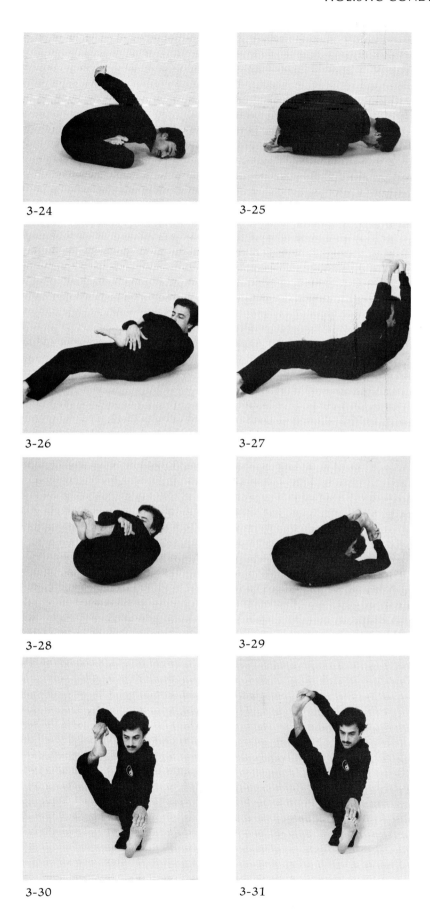

3-24

3-25

3-26

3-27

3-28

3-29

3-30

3-31

Time

Hold each leg for only a few seconds.

Asana 16: Shooting Arrow Pose (*Shanurasana*)

Technique

Sit on the floor, with legs stretching forward. Bend the right foot and catch hold of the left big toe with the right hand. Gently pull the right leg up until it touches the left ear. To "shoot the arrow," let go of the right foot and allow it to hit the left foot *(see photo 3-32.)*

Benefits

Flexibility and strength in the knee joint can result from this pose.

Time

Hold for a few seconds and "release the arrow."

Asana 17: The Candle (*Vrksana*)

This pose is sometimes called the tree.

Technique

Stand erect with hands down at your sides. Bring the right foot up and tuck it securely against the left thigh. Swing your arms in a wide arc to rest above the head, folded *(see photo 3-33)*.

Variation

Proceed as above, but stand on the toes.

Benefits

This pose tones the leg muscles and helps you develop a heightened sense of balance.

Time

Hold this pose for one to five minutes.

Asana 18: Lord of the Dance (Siva) Posture (*Natarajasana*)

Technique

Stand erect, raising the hands above the head. Bring your left foot up, bending the leg, and grasp it by the instep. At the same time, straighten and arch the back and raise the right arm as if holding up the sky *(see photo 3-34)*. After arching backward, lean forward, reach out with the right hand, and bring the left leg up in a bow position *(see photo 3-35)*.

Benefits

This pose promotes balance and mental calm.

Time

Hold for as long as is comfortable.

Asana 19: Extended Leg Posture (*Utthita Hasta Padangusthasana*)

Technique

Stand erect, with left leg up, holding on to the ball of the foot, and with the right arm extended at your side *(see photo 3-36)*. Extend the left leg, retaining your grip on the ball of the foot *(see photo 3-37)*.

Benefits

This pose provides improved balance and enhanced flexibility in the upper thigh area.

Time

Hold for as long as is comfortable.

Asana 20: Extended Leg Posture 2 (*Padangusthasana*)

Technique

Bring the right foot up to the groin area, holding the heel with the right arm and extending the left arm over the head *(see photo 3-38)*. Extend the right leg to the side, retaining your grip on the heel *(see photo 3-39)*.

3-32

3-33

3-34

3-35

3-36

3-37

3-38

3-39

Benefits

Balance and enhanced flexibility in the knee joint can result from this pose.

Time

Hold for as long as is comfortable.

Note: All yoga balance postures are essential in judo training since many throws require the *judoka* to balance on one leg.

Asana 21: Handstand

Technique

Place both hands on the floor and bring knees into the elbows. Center and raise the legs until a point of balance is achieved *(see photo 3-40).*

Variation

Do a standard handstand, except arch backward and extend one leg while bringing the other to the knee *(see photo 3-41).*

Benefits

The benefits of this pose are the same as those of the headstand, with the addition of increased strength in the upper arm and shoulder area and increased balance.

Time

Hold for up to five minutes, but *no longer.*

Asana 22: Leg Stretch Posture (*Supta Trivikramasana*)

Technique

Lie on your back. Extend your right leg upward and grasp it with the left hand *(see photo 3-42).* Bring the leg to the right side first *(see photo 3-43)* and then to the left side *(see photo 3-44).* Repeat with the left leg.

Benefits

This pose makes the legs extremely flexible. It also helps cure digestive disorders.

Time

Hold for one minute on each side.

Asana 23: Side Triangle Pose (*Utthita Trikonasana*)

Technique

Kneel on the floor and extend the left leg. Reach down to the left ankle with the left arm, bending from the waist *(see photo 3-45).*

Variation

From a standing position, bend down sideways with very little forward movement. Grasp the ankle *(see photo 3-46).*

Benefits

This pose promotes increased flexibility of side motion, which is essential to *koshi-waza* (hip-throwing) techniques. It also stretches the abdominal region, enhancing organ harmony.

Time

Hold for up to two minutes on each side.

Asana 24: Twist Position (*Ardha Matsyendrasana*)

Technique

Sit on the floor with both feet extended in front. Bring one leg up and reach the arm in between the bent leg and the straight leg. Twist to the side and bend the other knee to the buttocks *(see photo 3-47).*

Benefits

Superior spinal flexibility can be developed through this *asana.*

Time

Hold for up to ten minutes.

Asana 25: Cow Pose (*Gomukhasana*)

Technique

Cross one knee over the other and grasp your hands behind your back *(see photo 3-48).*

3-40

3-41

3-42

3-43

3-44

3-45

3-46

3-47

3-48

Benefits

This pose increases shoulder flexibility and expands the chest cavity for greater lung capacity.

Time

Hold for up to two minutes.

Asana 26: Locked Head-to-Knee Pose (*Maha Mudra*)

Technique

Sit with legs stretching forward. Gently grasp the left foot and place it on the right upper thigh. Reach around your back and grasp the left foot with the left hand. Grasp the big toe of the right foot with the right thumb and index finger. Bring the head down to the knee *(see photo 3-49)*. Repeat with the opposite leg.

Benefits

This pose improves general health and vitality (energy).

Time

Hold for as long as possible.

Asana 27: Leg-over-Head Pose (*Viranchyasana*)

Technique

Sit with legs stretched forward. Gently grasp the left leg, raising it over the head, and place it behind the head. Place palms against each other in front of your chest *(see photo 3-50)*.

Caution: Be sure not to force or strain the muscles or great damage will result.

Time

Hold for as long as is comfortable.

Asana 28: Tortoise Pose (*Koormasana*)

Technique

Sit with legs stretching forward. Spread them as far as they will go. Lift the knees slightly. Bend the trunk forward, bringing the head to the floor. One by one, insert the arms under the corresponding knees. Stretch the arms backward, with the palms facing up (for beginners) or down (for advanced students). Slowly bend forward until your chin touches the floor *(see photo 3-51)*.

Benefits

This pose is good for inner-thigh and lower-back flexibility. It also helps you develop a sense of calm.

Time

Hold for up to one minute.

Asana 29: Advanced Twist (*Parivrtta Janu Sirsasana*)

Technique

Assume Asana 9, grasp the ankle, and twist your body around until you can look up *(see photo 3-52)*.

Variation

Follow the standard method, but extend both legs *(see photo 3-53)*.

Benefits

See Asana 9. This pose also increases waist flexibility.

Asana 30: Back-Bending Bridge (*Urdhva Dhanurasana*)

Technique

Lie on your back with knees propped up and hands behind your shoulders. Lift your body up into a bridge position *(see photo 3-54)*.

Benefits

Spinal flexibility is improved by this posture.

Time

Hold for up to two minutes.

Asana 31: Wheel Posture (*Kapotasana*)

Techniques

Kneel on the floor and bend backward, supporting yourself by holding your ankles *(see photo 3-55)*.

Benefits

This pose expands the chest cavity and increases flexibility in the shoulder area.

Time

Hold for as long as desired.

3-49   3-50

3-51   3-52   3-53

3-54

3-55

Asana 32: The Sun Salute

The sun salute is the *best* all-around yoga conditioning exercise. It is superior for promoting flexibility and youth in the spine. The *judoka* should do at least five repetitions of it *daily*.

Technique

1. Stand erect and fold your hands over your chest *(see photo 3-56)*.
2. Bend backward *(see photo 3-57)*.
3. Bend forward *(see photo 3-58)*.
4. Step back with the left leg and form the standing bow posture *(see photo 3-59)*.
5. Place both hands on the floor and stretch backward, placing the buttocks in the air *(see photo 3-60)*.
6. Lie on the floor *(see photo 3-61)* . . .
7. . . . and form a cobra pose (Asana 6) *(see photo 3-62)*.
8. Return to the floor *(see photo 3-63)*.
9. Repeat step 5 *(see photo 3-64)*.
10. Step to the rear with the right foot and form the standing bow posture *(see photo 3-65)*.
11. Place the feet together and bend forward *(see photo 3-66)*.
12. Bend backward *(see photo 3-67)* . . .
13. . . . and return to step 1 *(see photo 3-68)*.

3-56

3-57

3-58

3-59

3-60

3-61

3-62

3-63

3-64

3-65

3-66

3-67

3-68

Asana 33: Meditative Postures

Posture 1: Easy Pose (Sukhasana)

Legs are folded comfortably under the knees (see photo 3-69).

Posture 2: Half Lotus

Heels are placed under the groin area—first the left heel and then the right heel. Knees should rest on the floor (see photo 3-70).

Posture 3: Full Lotus (Padmasana)

Rest the right foot on the left thigh and then the left foot on the right thigh (see photo 3-71).

Posture 4: Kneeling Pose (Vajrasana)

Kneel, keeping the back straight (see photo 3-72).

3-69

3-70

3-71

3-72

PRANAYAMA—YOGIC BREATHING

One of the most important factors in our body's energy production is breath. As oxygen enters the body it provides the fundamental fuel for the metabolic activities of the cells. The energy supplied by the respiratory process affects the functioning of the brain, our stamina, and our basic well-being.

Thus: Food + Oxygen = Energy. Therefore, the *judoka* who takes a holistic approach to his training by eating correctly (see Appendix II) and breathing correctly will have greater energy and stamina than a *judoka* who takes a halfhearted approach.

Breath control is therefore an integral part of judo advancement. The mind and body are the instruments through which we receive all our experience. Thus, the inner connection among breathing, mind, and body is very important. Example: When one is sitting idle, breathing slows down; suspension of mental activity increases in proportion to the slowing down of the breath. On the other hand, if we are tense, or afraid, our breathing is shallow and quick.

Therefore, the regulation of harmonized breathing helps one to achieve regulation and steadiness of mind. Conversely, by controlling the mind you also control the vital breathing.

Vital breathing, or *pranayama*, as it is called in yoga, is the method of taking in *prana*, the life energy that vitalizes all living things and controls the activities of the body—physical, mental, and spiritual. Without it, blood won't circulate, organs won't do their job, and so on.

The concept of a universal energy force is not something that should be put in the realm of the "mystical" and forgotten about. Nearly all cultures have taught this concept by different names: *mana* (Polynesians), *ki* (Japanese, as in aikido) *chi* (Chinese, as in Tai *Chi* Chuan), and *ruach* (Hebrew for "spirit of life"). A more contemporary term is *bioplasma*, recently coined by many scientists.

Prana is most easily absorbed into the body through the air, where it is found in its freest state (many cultures consider "air" itself

prana). As you perform judo, you are inhaling, with each breath, air charged with this force. Like an electric current, it courses through the body to every muscle and organ, renewing strength and vigor.

For those who cannot accept the theory of *prana*, the practice of *pranayama* is still very beneficial, since through it one takes in more oxygen and thus more energy for competitive training.

Judo recognizes four forms of breathing: high, mid, low, and complete.

High Breathing

High breathing involves raising the shoulders and collarbone while the abdomen is contracted. Neither the diaphragm nor the rib muscles are used. Most people—especially those who are not very physically active—are high breathers. The problem with high breathing, as it relates to judo, is that the air intake is so shallow that it is very hard to catch your breath to restore the necessary vigor.

Mid-Breathing

Mid-breathing (chest breathing) does not involve the diaphragm but instead the intercostal muscles of the rib cage. This breathing is done entirely through the actions of these muscles. Chest breathing commonly occurs during physical work or intense judo *randori* exercise. The stomach will become very tense. Only about half the lung is used in this breathing pattern.

Low Breathing

Low breathing (the best of the three), uses the action of the diaphragm. The lungs are employed far more extensively in low breathing than in mid-or high breathing. They fill about three-quarters full.

To find out for yourself which of the three ways is best, count the number of seconds you take to fill the lungs. You will note that low breathing brings more air to the lungs with less effort than the other two types of breathing. But mid-breathing is better than high breathing. High breathing is the worst of all breaths (and yet is the most common among non-yoga-trained *judoka*). High breathers use the most energy to get the *least air*.

Complete Breathing

The best breathing is the yogic complete breath. This involves using simultaneously all three types of breathing mentioned thus far, starting with low breathing, continuing to chest breathing, and finishing with high breathing.

1. Inhale slowly, using the diaphragm as in deep breathing. Aim the breath below the stomach and notice the stomach bulging out. This will fill the lower part of the lungs with air.
2. Continue to breathe and fill the mid-section by expanding the rib section outward to the sides.
3. Finally, fill the uppermost part of the lungs by lifting up the chest area as in high breathing.
4. Hold for eight to ten seconds.
5. Begin exhalation by gently contracting the lower stomach. This will push air out of the lower lungs, which will make the chest muscles relax and the shoulder muscles relax, forcing all air out. Pause a few seconds before doing it again.

In complete breathing, the greatest attention is paid to the process of exhalation; the time ratio between inhalation and exhalation is 1:2. Thus, if it takes you one second to inhale, take two seconds to exhale. This allows you to get maximum control of the lungs, letting the sacs filled with stale air to empty (in regular exhalation you empty only about three-quarters of the air).

Therefore, the first step in complete breathing is starting 1:2. After properly establishing the inhalation/exhalation cycle, the next step is to retain the breath proportionately. The ratio between inhalation and retention is 1:4. Since the retention is four times the length of the inhalation, and exhalation is always twice inhalation, the new ratio in 1:4:2.

Pranayama Exercise 1: Alternate Nostril Breathing
Technique

Sit comfortably in a meditative posture (see "Asana 33: Meditative Postures") and rest your left hand in the middle of your lap. Follow these steps:

1. Close the right nostril with your right thumb *(see photo 3-73)*
2. Slowly inhale the complete breath through the left nostril and hold the breath for 10 counts.
3. With the knuckle of the middle finger on your right hand, close the left nostril and hold the breath for 10 counts *(see photo 3-74).*
4. Exhale by releasing only the thumb and slowly exhale through the right nostril for 10 counts.
5. Pause for two counts.
6. Keeping the right nostril open, slowly inhale the total breath for 10 counts.
7. Now close the right nostril with the thumb and hold the breath for 10 counts.
8. Exhale through the left nostril for 10 counts by releasing the middle knuckle only.
9. Pause for two counts. Continue the breath by alternating the nostrils until you have inhaled 10 times through each (for beginners, five times through each).

After finishing this *pranayama* you will feel a sense of calm throughout the body as well as a great sense of revitalization.

Pranayama 2: Restraint Breathing (*Uddiyana Bandha*)
Technique

Stand relaxed and follow these instructions:

1. Stoop over slightly, bending the knees and placing your hands on your thighs (fingers spread).
2. Lower your chin until it rests on the spot between the collarbone and the breastbone.

3. Inhale deeply and then exhale quickly so that the air is forced out of the body in a rush.
4. Hold the breath. Pull the whole abdominal region back toward the spine. Contract the abdominal muscles and lift it up toward the breastbone, pressing the hands against the thighs *(see photo 3-75)*.
5. Relax the abdominal muscles, but don't move the chin and head.
6. Inhale slowly and deeply. Exhale.

Pranayama 3: Restraint Breathing ? (Nauli)

Technique

In addition to increasing the body's ability to take in oxygen, this *pranayama* has the added benefits of toning the stomach muscles in addition to removing toxins and waste from the abdominal region. Follow these steps:

1. Assume the same basic starting posture as in Pranayama 2.
2. Perform the *uddiyana bandha* (Pranayama 2).
3. After the abdomen is sucked in, hold the position and physically and mentally create a passive area between the pelvic rim and the floating ribs on both sides of the abdomen. When this passive relaxation is accomplished, push the abdominal recti forward *(see photo 3-76)*.
4. Maintain the position for 5–10 seconds.
5. Relax the grip on the recti and go back to the *uddiyana bandha* position.
6. Come out of *uddiyana bandha* by following steps 5 and 6 from Pranayama 2.

3-73

3-74

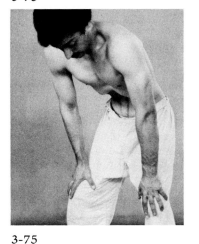

3-75

3-76

JUDO BREATHING EXERCISES

In addition to yogic *pranayama*, a solid judo conditioning program should concentrate on active breathing exercises. Active breathing exercises have two different purposes: (1) they are the actual methods of breathing used in the execution of techniques *or* (2) they are methods of breathing used to build strength and stamina in the *judoka*.

Breathing that builds strength is called *ibuki* breathing; breathing used during the execution of techniques is *nogare* breathing.

Ibuki Breathing

Ibuki breathing helps you master body tension and teaches you to concentrate your strength. It is a principle of physics that the greatest force will be developed by the body at the point when half of the lung's capacity has been expelled.

Ibuki is accomplished through these steps:

1. Stand in a *jigotai* posture, with hands crossed over the groin *(see photo 3-77)*.
2. Inhale deeply, using mid and high breathing, at the same time raising the arms to expand the chest and crossing the forearms over your head as you lean back slightly *(see photo 3-78)*.
3. Exhale sharply, throwing the arms down and tensing the stomach muscles. (*Note:* In karate, the mouth is open and the breath is sharp, sometimes done with a *kiai* (shout); in judo, the exhalation is still done through the mouth, but it remains half-closed almost as if throwing a kiss. Remember, the breath whistles through the mouth.) *(See photo 3-79.)*

Nogare Breathing

This method of breathing is used during the execution of judo techniques and in *randori* (free fighting) in order to maintain composure and control. The breath comes in the nostrils deeply and quietly, is held for a few moments, and then is exhaled through the mouth in a composed and controlled fashion. The tongue is placed behind the teeth on the roof of the mouth to keep the breath soft and quiet.

Nogare Breathing 1

1. Extend your arms and act as if you are lifting a heavy object, at the same time executing low breathing through the nose *(see photo 3-80)*.
2. Without hesitation, continue the movement of the arms, raising them up under the armpits. This will expand the chest for mid and high breathing. By the time the hands come up under the armpits the *judoka* will have executed the yogic complete breath *(see photo 3-81)*.
3. Exhale through the mouth quietly, lowering the hands as if pressing down a hard object *(see photo 3-82)*.

Nogare Breathing 2

1. This *nogare* breathing uses mid-breathing exclusively. Simply start with the hands at the sides, palms facing forward. Inhale with the chest *(see photo 3-83)*.
2. Raise the arms up under the armpits while inhaling to expand the chest for more air *(see photo 3-84)*.
3. Exhale, tensing the stomach muscles and arm/shoulder muscles with the palms pressing downward *(see photo 3-85)*.

Kiai (Shouting)

In short, a *kiai* is a shout, a piercing sound made at the completion of either *ibuki* or *nogare* breathing. It is intended to give more "psych" and power to a given technique or to stun and throw off an opponent's attempted attack.

The shout must be generated from the lower abdomen to gain the greatest effect. It will increase the confidence of the *judoka* as well as decrease the confidence of the attacker. *Kiais* are often used in give-and-take practice on executing the throw as well as on receiving (taking the fall). I have found that a

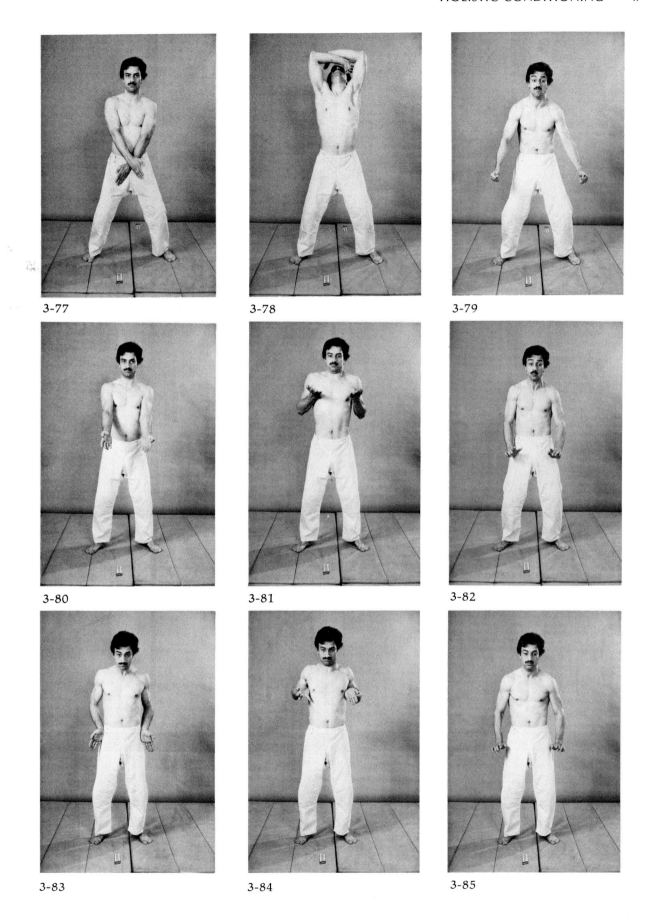

3-77

3-78

3-79

3-80

3-81

3-82

3-83

3-84

3-85

strong *kiai* on hitting the mat will empty the lungs, making the *judoka* feel the fall less and decreasing the chance of having the "wind knocked out of him."

CONDITIONING EXERCISE FOR STRENGTH AND FLEXIBILITY

Judo has many conditioning exercises that are unique to the art, in addition to some that are rather standard. I have illustrated only those that I have found helpful over the years.

Judo Push-Ups

Push-Up 1

1. Place feet far apart, with palms on the mat at shoulder width *(see photo 3-86)*.
2. Bring the body down to the mat: first the chin *(see photo 3-87)*, then the chest, and finally . . .
3. . . . the lower abdomen *(see photo 3-88)*. The push-up is, in fact, done with a rocking motion.

Push-Up 2

1. This push-up is done like the traditional method except it is performed on the knuckles (first two only). Keep the back straight and the buttocks down *(see photo 3-89)*.
2. Bring the chin to the floor and back to position 1 *(see photo 3-90)*.

Push-Up 3

This is the same as Push-Up 2, but it is done on the wrists *(see photo 3-91)*.

Push-Up 4

This is the same as Push-Up 2, but it is done on the fingertips *(see photo 3-92)*.

Leg Raisers

It is best to perform leg raisers at three angles: first at a 90-degree angle to the floor *(see photo 3-93)*; second, at a 45-degree angle *(see photo 3-94)*; and last, from a couple of inches off the floor *(see photo 3-95)*.

Note: You can hold them for any length of time. Beginners hold them for about 15 seconds each, black belts up to one minute at each stage.

3-86

3-87

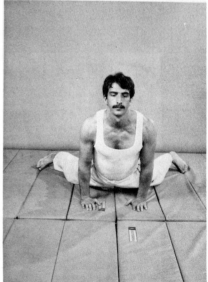

3-88

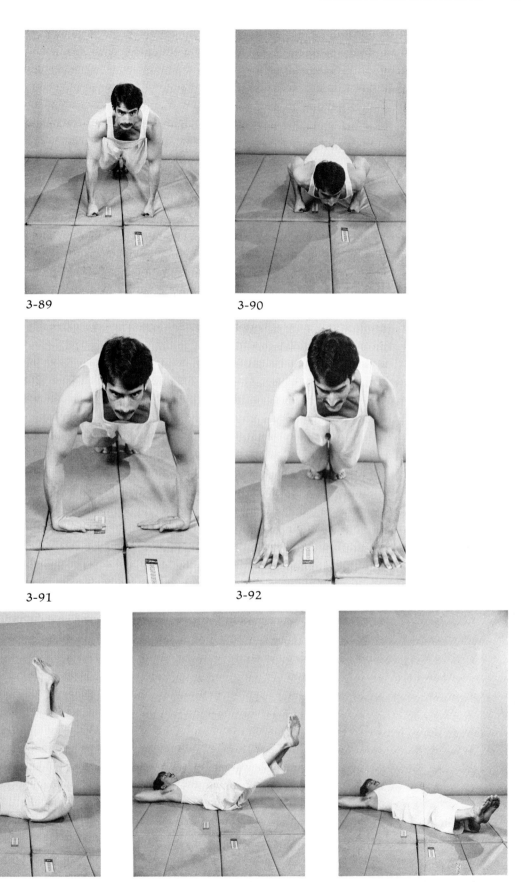

3-89

3-90

3-91

3-92

3-93

3-94

3-95

Sit-Ups

Sit-Up 1

1. Lie on your back with knees up and hands folded behind the neck *(see photo 3-96)*.
2. Bring yourself up to a position halfway to the knees and hold for several seconds *(see photo 3-97)*. This develops the abdominal muscles better than the traditional Sit-Up.

Sit-Up 2

1. Lie on your back, hands folded behind the neck and legs supported by a partner *(see photo 3-98)*.
2. Bring yourself up to your knees with a *smooth*, nonjerking motion *(see photo 3-99)*. This is an excellent Sit-Up for *upper* abdominal muscles.

Sit-Up 3

1. Sit on your partner's back with hands folded behind your neck *(see photo 3-100)*.
2. Arch your back toward your partner's head.

3. Bring your elbows to your partner's buttocks *(see photo 3-101)*.

Leg Squats

Pick your partner up on your shoulders in a fireman's carry *(see photo 3-102)*. Keep your back straight and bend up and down from the knees *(see photo 3-103)*. Do about 10 reps when beginning and up to 50 reps when advanced.

Knee Rotations

1. Stand on your toes and keep your hands on your knees *(see photo 3-104)*.
2. Rotate your knees counterclockwise *(see photo 3-105)* . . .
3. . . . until straight *(see photo 3-106)*.
4. Repeat, going clockwise.

Ankle Pops

1. Stand on your toes with your feet together and your arms outstretched in front of you *(see photo 3-107)*.
2. Snap toe to heel, at the same time putting hands on hips *(see photo 3-108)*.

Note: This exercise is excellent for improving balance and strengthening the ankles.

  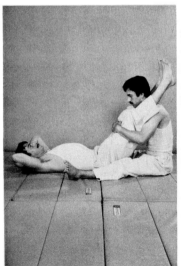 

3-96   3-97   3-98   3-99

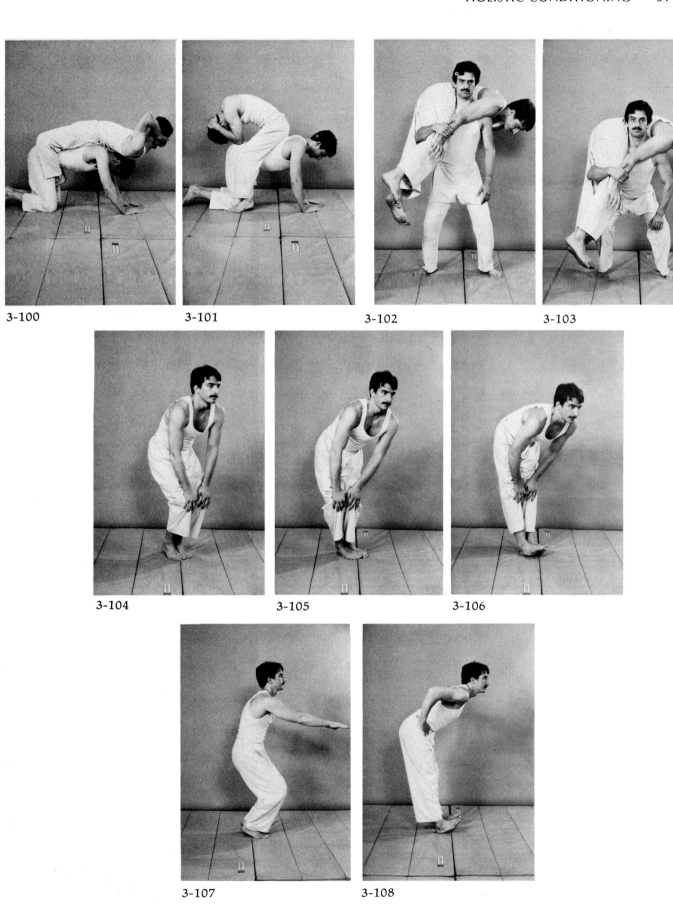

3-100   3-101   3-102   3-103

3-104   3-105   3-106

3-107   3-108

Squats

This is an excellent exercise for strengthening the knees and stretching the legs and groin muscles.

1. Stand in a *jigotai* posture *(see photo 3-109)*.
2. Keeping hands on hips, squat to the right *(see photo 3-110)*.
3. Then squat to the left *(see photo 3-111)*.

Ankle Rotations

This exercise is intended to loosen the ankle and inner thigh muscles.

1. Start by stretching the leg muscles with the foot firmly planted on the mat *(see photo 3-112)*.
2. Rotate the ankle until the toes are pointed straight up *(see photo 3-113)*.
3. Stretch forward by placing the head on the knee *(see photo 3-114)*.
4. Repeat with the other leg.

Hurdler Stretch

This is excellent for loosening the leg, knee, and back muscles prior to a judo workout.

1. Bend one leg with the knee pointing forward and the foot backward. Place the other leg out straight, resting on the mat *(see photo 3-115)*. Touch your head to the knee of the straight leg.
2. Reverse the stretching action by lying down on the mat with the leg still in the cocked position *(see photo 3-116)*.

Leg Thrusts

This is a good exercise for developing strong legs and flexible knees.

1. Lie on the mat with your head *up*, your legs bent and off the floor, and your hands locked behind the neck *(see photo 3-117)*.
2. Kick first with the right leg *(see photo 3-118)*.
3. Then kick with the left *(see photo 3-119)*. The kicks must be fast and continuous, never stopping. Do 200–500 repetitions per workout.

Forward Two-Man Stretching

This is a good exercise to loosen your back and groin muscles. Because there is a second *judoka* involved, the forward motion adds weight to help in stretching the muscles faster.

3-109

3-110

3-111

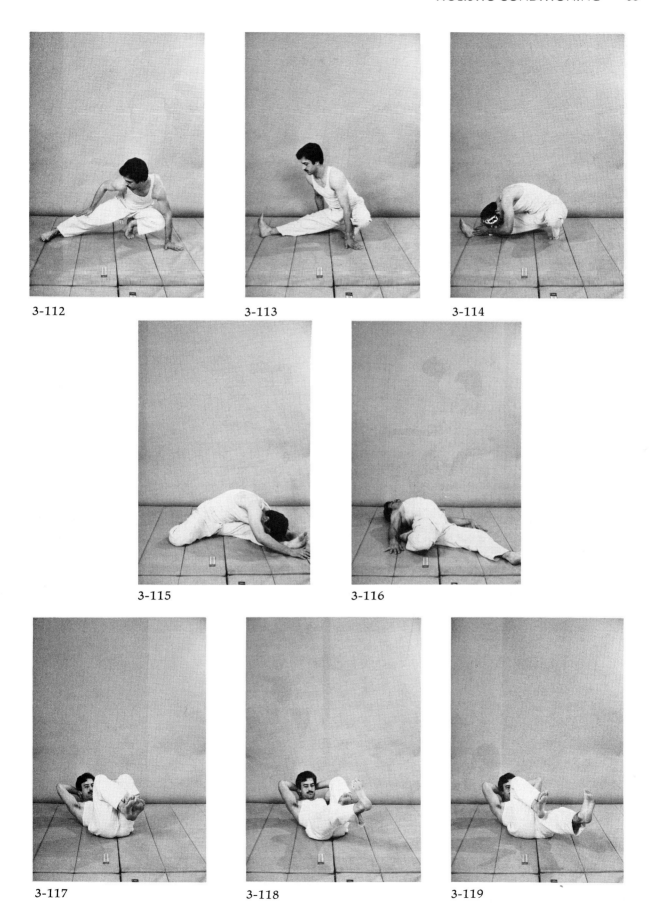

3-112

3-113

3-114

3-115

3-116

3-117

3-118

3-119

1. Both *judoka* place their feet as far apart as they can and grasp hands *(see photo 3-120)*.
2. As one player leans back and rests his back on the mat, the partner is stretched forward *(see photo 3-121)*.
3. Repeat by having the other partner lie back.

Neck Strengthening and Flexibility Exercises

Flexibilty Exercises

1. Rotate your head clockwise in a complete circle, starting by placing the head to the right side *(see photo 3-122)*.
2. Rotate it to the back position *(see photo 3-123)*.
3. Now rotate to the left side *(see photo 3-124)*.
4. Finally, rotate it forward *(see photo 3-125)*.

One-Man Strengthening Exercise

1. Stretch by looking to the left *(see photo 3-126)*.
2. Then look to the right *(see photo 3-127)*.
3. With the aid of both hands, press the head back *(see photo 3-128)*.
4. Then press forward *(see photo 3-129)*.

Two-Man Strengthening Exercise

These exercises are intended for use only after the *judoka* has been doing the single-man neck exercise for a few months.

1. *Side Strengthening:* Have your partner lie on his side and press against the side of his head as the partner resists the pressing *(see photo 3-130)*. Repeat to the other side.
2. *Forward Strengthening:* Lie on your back and have your partner press against your forehead as you resist *(see photo 3-131)*.

Belt Exercises

Single Flexibility Exercises

These exercises are intended to loosen the groin muscles for better extension on throws that involve lifting a leg. The belt is used like a pulley to draw the leg up. An added benefit of the exercises is improved balance.

1. Wrap the belt securely in each hand and step into the center of the loop.
2. Draw the belt up until the leg is fully extended *(see photo 3-132)*.
3. After extending it fully forward, repeat with the other leg.
4. Now step once again into the loop, but this time draw your leg to the side with a slight forward bias until it is fully extended *(see photo 3-133)*.
5. Bring the leg down and repeat with the opposite leg.

3-120

3-121

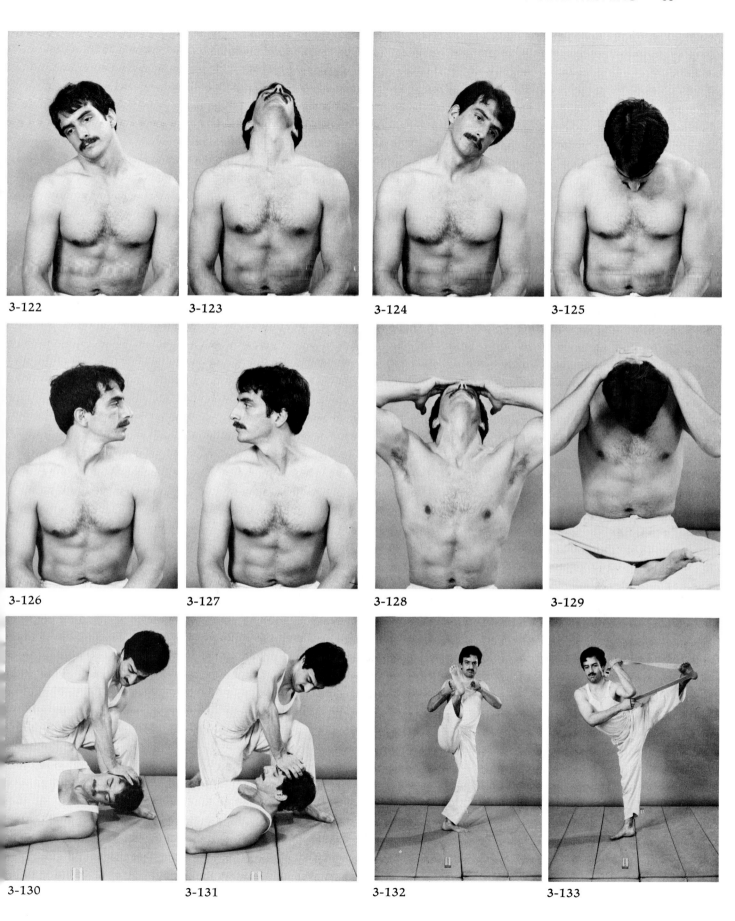

3-122   3-123   3-124   3-125

3-126   3-127   3-128   3-129

3-130   3-131   3-132   3-133

Single Strength Exercises

In reality these are nothing more than isometric exercises done with a judo belt.

1. Start by placing the belt under the foot, locking the knee and pulling with all your strength *(see photo 3-134)*. Remember, these are isometric exercises, so *do not* move the leg.
2. Relax. Place the belt under the opposite leg and pull.
3. Relax. Place the belt behind the head and pull apart and forward *(see photo 3-135)*.
4. Relax. Place the belt under the buttocks, squat, and pull up *(see photo 3-136)*. Relax.

Two-Man Strengthening Exercises

These are tug-of-war-type exercises, in which one person holds the belt on specific body parts of his partner and each tries to pull the other over an imaginary line drawn between them. When one person crosses it, the pulling ceases and the other person gives it a try. Exercises are done by pulling against the waist *(see photo 3-137)*, against the neck *(see photo 3-138)*, or against the leg *(see photo 3-139)*.

Isometric Exercises

Judo also has its own isometric exercises that do not involve a belt.

1. Stand in the *jigotai* posture with hands together and fingers pointed down *(see photo 3-140)*.
2. Strain by placing palm to palm and trying to fuse them together *(see photo 3-141)*.
3. Relax. Return the palms to the center of the chest, but this time fingers should be pointed to the sky *(see photo 3-142)*.
4. Press the palms together, at the same time raising them into the air *(see photo 3-143)*.
5. Relax. Rest the hands down in front of you and imagine that the wrists are bound by rope, handcuffs, etc. *(see photo 3-144)*.
6. Strain by trying to separate the wrists *(see photo 3-145)*. Relax.

UKEMI-WAZA: BREAKFALL TECHNIQUES

The first rule in judo is: *Be prepared to fall.* Even if you are doing the throwing, it is always possible to be countered and find yourself hitting the mat. *Ukemi-waza*, or breakfall techniques, are perhaps the most fundamentally important conditioning exercise to be learned in judo. For it is *ukemi-waza* that trains you to take falls without getting hurt.

Falling must become a reflex action. One

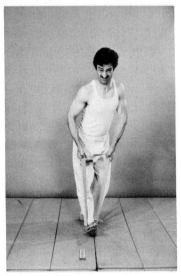
3-134

3-135

3-136

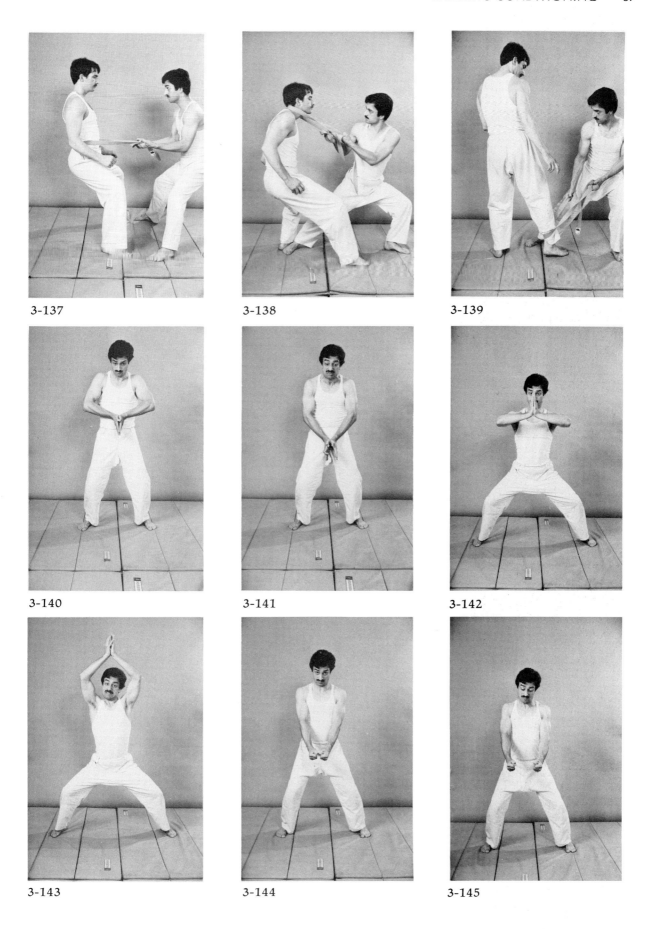

3-137

3-138

3-139

3-140

3-141

3-142

3-143

3-144

3-145

can't think about how to fall; one simply must fall—and fall perfectly. The only exercises for this are *practice* and *meditation*. One must *think* (meditate) with proper visualization on how to fall and develop the confidence to do it right. He must also *do it* constantly, even after attaining high-ranking black belts. Before each judo workout I still do 15 minutes of breakfalls, and I also make a potential *judoka* train exclusively in breakfalls for three or four weeks before he learns anything else.

Ura-Ukemi (Rear Breakfalls)

This breakfall is done in three stages: sitting, standing, and leaping.

Sitting

Sit on the mat with feet extended, hands resting on the knees, back arched, and the chin resting on the chest *(see photo 3-146)*. Roll backward and at the same time slap the mat with both hands *(see photo 3-147)*.

Important points: (1) Slap *hard* to absorb the energy of the fall. (2) Keep the tailbone off the mat surface. (3) Keep the head off the mat surface.

Standing

Extend the left foot and extend the arms out in front of the body *(see photo 3-148)*. Bend down to touch your toes *(see photo 3-149)*, at the same time rolling on your back and slapping *(see photo 3-150)*.

Leaping

This is similar to standing, except you start with feet together and hands crossed in front of the chest *(see photo 3-151)*. Leap from the knees into the air *(see photo 3-152)* and land in a perfect sitting posture *(see photo 3-153)*.

Yoko-Ukemi (Side Breakfall)

This is perhaps the single most important breakfall since it is used nine times out of 10 when one is receiving a fall. It has three classifications: lying, standing, and leaping.

Lying

Lie on the mat with head *up* and feet extended forward. Place your left arm over your face *(see photo 3-154)*. Rotate to the left side, at the same time *slapping* the mat with both the left hand and the feet *(see photo 3-155)*. The feet come up slightly and then are brought down with one foot tucked in toward the other with the sole of the foot down *(see close-up photo 3-156)*.

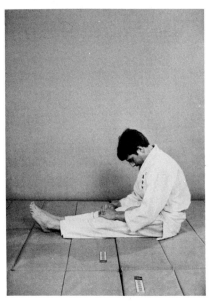

3-146

3-147

3-148

3-149

3-150

3-151

3-152

3-153

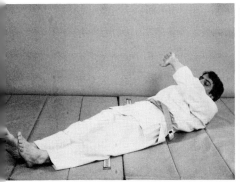

-154

3-155

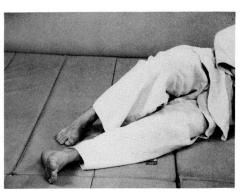

3-156

Standing

From a standing position, raise your leg and your hand simultaneously *(see photo 3-157)*. Bring yourself gently down to the mat and slap, at the same time drawing your legs up into the air *(see photo 3-158)*.

Leaping

This is similar to standing, but one sweeps the legs into the air *(see photos 3-159, 3-160)*, becomes airborne, and slaps the mat, keeping the legs up high *(see photos 3-161, 3-162)*.

Mae-Ukemi (Front Breakfall)

This breakfall is useful when a potential throw is countered by your opponent and you find yourself flying into the mat face first. This breakfall has three parts: kneeling, standing, and leaping.

Kneeling

Kneel erect, arms out at the sides, with elbows bent and palms facing forward *(see photo 3-163)*. Fall forward, slapping the mat with the palms and forearms simultaneously *(see photo 3-164)*.

Standing

Stand erect with palms facing forward *(see photo 3-165)*. Begin falling forward *(see photo 3-166)* until contact is made with the mat. Both arms must strike at the same time *(see photo 3-167)*.

Leaping

Stand on your toes with both feet together, hands crossed over chest *(see photo 3-168)*. Leap into the air *(see photo 3-169)* looking forward, not straight down. When impact occurs, be sure to strike the mat with both hands (palms and forearms) at the same time *(see photo 3-170)*.

Forward/Backward Rolling

These are breakfalls in their own right (in *jujutsu*) but are used in judo as conditioning exercises for the *zempo kaiten ukemi* (forward rolling breakfalls).

3-157

3-158

3-159

3-160

3-161

3-162

3-163

3-164

3-165

3-166

3-167

3-168

3-169

3-170

Forward Roll

Wrap your hands on top of your head to protect it *(see photo 3-171)*. Roll by placing the arms on the mat *(see photo 3-172)*, and rolling forward until you come back onto your feet *(see photo 3-173)*.

Rear Somersault

Squat with hands extended and ready at the side of the head *(see photo 3-174)*. Roll backward and come up on the extended palms *(see photo 3-175)*. Use the hands to protect the neck and help you roll back onto your feet *(see photo 3-176)*.

Zempo Kaiten Ukemi (Forward Rolling Breakfall)

This breakfall puts practical use to the lying *yoko-ukemi*. In reality, *zempo kaiten* gives one the ability to take a throw. This breakfall can be broken into many different parts. We will illustrate squatting, standing, and leaping.

Squatting

This is perhaps the single most important breakfall because it develops strength and puts to use the *yoko-ukemi*. Start squatting with one hand pointed ahead (corresponding to the side on which you will fall) and one hand tucked in (corresponding to the shoulder on which you will roll). The hands can form a triangle (not essential, but a good way to start) *(see photo 3-177)*. Begin to roll, keeping yourself *tight (see photo 3-178)*. Land in a *yoko-ukemi (see photo 3-179)*.

Standing

This is the same as squatting, but you begin from a standing position *(see photo 3-180)*, roll onto the shoulder *(see photo 3-181)*, keep yourself tight *(see photo 3-182)*, and land in *yoko-ukemi (see photo 3-183)*.

3-171

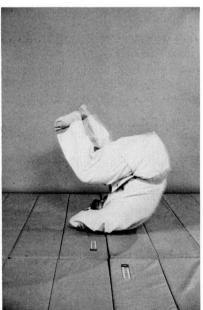
3-172

3-173

3-174

3-175

3-176

3-177

3-178

3-179

3-180

3-181

3-182

3-183

Leaping

This variation can be done with either hands touching the mat or a complete flip into *yoko-ukemi*. Begin in a composed standing posture *(see photo 3-184)*. Step forward *(see photo 3-185)* and leap into the air *(see photo 3-186)*, landing in a *yoko-ukemi (see photo 3-187)*.

Raised Back Breakfall

Again, this breakfall is used more in *jujutsu* than in judo, but it has saved my neck (literally) a number of times in competition, so I have included it. It can be done squatting or leaping.

Squatting

Squat on all fours *(see photo 3-188)*. Roll over, *but do not let your head touch the mat.* Use your arms to keep it off the mat *(see photo 3-189)*. Fall to the back by letting both feet hit the mat at the same time the shoulders do *(see photo 3-190)*.

Important Points: (1) Keep the buttocks off the mat. (2) Keep the head up. (3) Be sure to slap with the hands.

Leaping

Stand with one foot forward and hands crossed over your chest *(see photo 3-191)*. Lean onto one foot *(see photo 3-192)* and somersault completely over *without* touching the head to the mat *(see photo 3-193)*. Land as described above *(see photo 3-194)*.

3-184   3-185   3-186   3-187

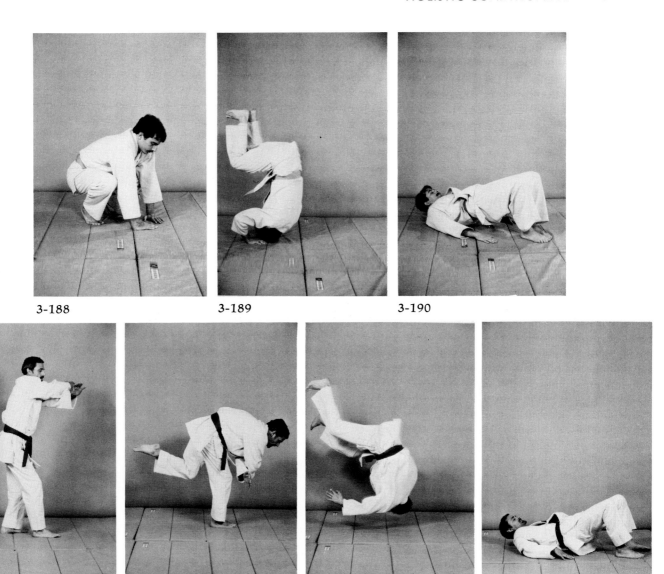

3-188   3-189   3-190

3-191   3-192   3-193   3-194

4
NAGE-WAZA
(THROWING TECHNIQUES)

Throwing techniques make up the solid foundation of modern judo. Although they represent only a small portion of all judo techniques, much time is spent on perfecting them, long after one achieves black belt.

The judo throw looks deceptively simple, especially if done correctly. The throws are also extremely beautiful; a perfectly executed throw is a genuine work of performing art.

This chapter will examine the forty basic throwing techniques referred to as *Gokyo-no-waza* (Techniques of Five). Although they are forty in number, their variations and alterations could run well into the thousands.

When learning throwing techniques it is best to start slow and concentrate on each part. As Bruce Lee said, "When I learned a technique, it was just a technique; when I got more familiar with it, it was no longer a technique; when I mastered it, it was just a technique." One can interpret this to mean: when you learn a technique, watch the entire thing until it is a working whole; when you know it, break it apart and master each piece; and when it is mastered, put it back together again to form a working whole.

The following are some tips to follow in executing the techniques:

1. *Stay centered* (see Chapter 2).
2. *Stay grounded* (see Chapter 2).
3. Keep good, close body contact.
4. Relax. Do not perform the techniques while stiff.
5. Grip should be tight but relaxed.
6. Keep the back straight and do not bend it until you are ready to execute the throw.

The *Gokyo-no-waza*, or "Techniques of Five," are five sets of throws consisting of eight throws per set (forty altogether). Many organizations base rank on the execution of each set. These groups award a black belt when all forty throws are mastered (along with other techniques, of course). The *Gokyo-no-waza* are as follows:

DAI IK KYO NO WAZA (Set 1)

1. *De Ashi Barai*—Advanced Foot Sweep
2. *Hiza Guruma*—Knee Wheel
3. *Sasae Tsuri-komi Ashi*—Lift-and-Pull Ankle Throw

4. *Uki-goshi*—Floating Hip Throw
5. *Osoto Gari*—Major Outer Leg Sweep
6. *Ogoshi*—Major Hip Throw
7. *Ouchi Gari*—Major Inner Leg Sweep
8. *Seoinage*—Shoulder Throw.

DAI NI KYO NO WAZA (Set 2)

1. *Ko Soto Gari*—Minor Outer Leg Sweep
2. *Ko Uchi Gari*—Minor Inner Leg Sweep
3. *Koshi Guruma*—Hip Wheel
4. *Tsuri Komi-goshi*—Lift-and-Pull Hip Throw
5. *Okuri Ashi Harai*—Sweeping Ankle Throw
6. *Tai-otoshi*—Body Drop
7. *Harai-goshi*—Sweeping Hip Throw
8. *Uchi Mata*—Inner Thigh Throw

DAI SAN KYO NO WAZA (Set 3)

1. *Ko Soto Gake*—Minor Outer Hooking Ankle Throw
2. *Tsuri-goshi*—Lifting Hip Throw
3. *Yoko-otoshi*—Side Drop
4. *Ashi Guruma*—Leg Wheel
5. *Hane-Goshi*—Spring Hip Throw
6. *Harai Tsuri Komi Ashi*—Sweeping Drawing Ankle Throw
7. *Tomoe Nage*—Circle Throw
8. *Kata Guruma*—Shoulder Wheel

DAI YON KYO NO WAZA (Set 4)

1. *Sumi Gaeshi*—Corner Throw
2. *Tani-otoshi*—Valley Drop
3. *Hane Maki-komi*—Outer Winding Spring Throw
4. *Sukui Nage*—Scooping Throw
5. *Utsuri-goshi*—Changing Hip Throw
6. *O-guruma*—Major Wheel
7. *Soto Maki-komi*—Major Outer Winding Throw
8. *Uki-otoshi*—Floating Drop

DAI GO KYO NO WAZA (Set 5)

1. *O Soto Guruma*—Major Outer Wheel
2. *Uki Waza*—Floating Throw
3. *Yoko Wakare*—Side Separation
4. *Yoko Guruma*—Side Wheel
5. *Ushiro-goshi*—Rear Hip Throw
6. *Ura Nage*—Rear Throw
7. *Sumi-otoshi*—Corner Drop
8. *Yoko Gake*—Side Hooking Throw

Each throw will be explained in detail, with the following aspects covered for each:

Description: A description of the throw, with history, meaning, and purpose (where available).
Execution:

1. *Kuzushi*—the steps in off-balancing.
2. *Tsukuri*—the steps of moving in after the act of throwing him off balance.
3. *Kake*—the execution of the throw itself.

Special Hints (if any)
Alternate Throws: Throws that are next best to use when the first throw fails.
Defenses: Countering techniques, explained only for the major competition throws.

SET 1: *DAI IK KYO NO WAZA*

1. De Ashi Barai

Description

The throw is classified as a leg throw (*ashi-waza*) because the action of the throw comes from the use of the legs. It is an excellent throw to apply on an advancing opponent when his weight is placed forward.

Execution

1. *Kuzuki:* Force the opponent (left, in photos) to step forward *(see photo 4-1)* by pulling him forward with the left arm and backward with the right arm *(see photo 4-2)*. His weight is not completely on the forward leg (because of your pushing backward) and is very vulnerable.

2. *Tsukuri:* As you are applying the *kuzushi*, step slightly to the rear with the left foot and bring your left foot to his right ankle *(see photo 4-3)*.

3. *Kake:* Draw the sole of your foot diagonally across the mat and catch your opponent's ankle *(see close-up photo 4-4)* pulling him straight down with your left hand and straight back and down with your right hand *(see photos 4-5, 4-6)*.

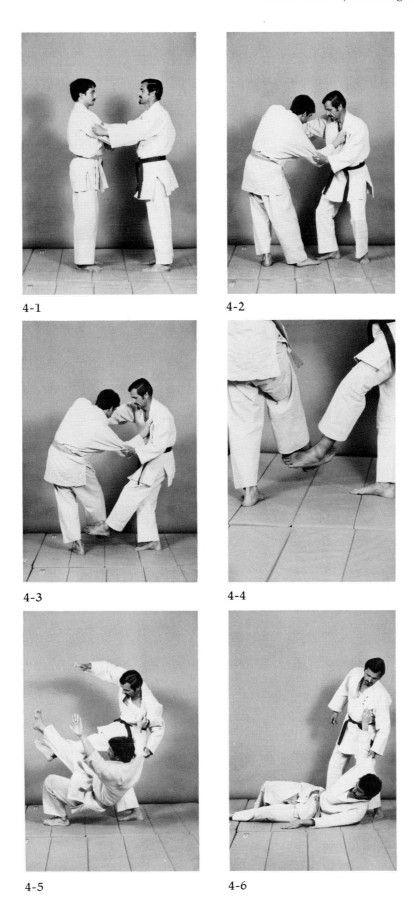

4-1

4-2

4-3

4-4

4-5

4-6

Special Hints

Pull hard with your left arm to bring the opponent's foot forward and to the *inside* of your legs. When sweeping, always think beyond the object that you are sweeping so your foot keeps going.

Alternate Throws

Tani-otoshi and *Yoko-otoshi* are both good.

Defenses

As the opponent sweeps *(see photo 4-7),* lift your foot so his passes by *(see photo 4-8)* and continue with a sweep of your own *(see photo 4-9).* Since the opponent has committed himself to a strong sweeping action, it will be very easy to take him down— *but perfect timing is essential.*

2. Hiza Guruma

Description

A very difficult throw to time, the Knee Wheel, also an *ashi-waza* technique, is performed by bracing your nonsupported foot under the opponent's kneecap and swinging the opponent right around it to the ground.

Execution

1. *Kuzushi:* Stand together and take two or three *tsugi-ashi* (see Chapter 2) steps to the rear. The opponent (left, in photos) will have to follow suit. When he does, and his legs are farther apart, pull him forward to force him to put all his weight on the forward leg *(see photos 4-10, 4-11).*

2. *Tsukuri:* Now that the opponent's weight is on his forward leg, place the sole of your foot under his kneecap *(see photo 4-12). Note:* Be careful to place it *under* the kneecap so as not to injure your opponent *(see close-up photo 4-13).*

3. *Kake:* Pull around, using the arms and the entire body in a big twist but not moving the blocking foot, which takes the opponent down in a large arch *(see photos 4-14, 4-15).*

Special Hints

Use strong pulling actions and a complete *twisting action* of the waist. *Note:* Do not twist so much that you lose your balance.

4-7   4-8   4-9

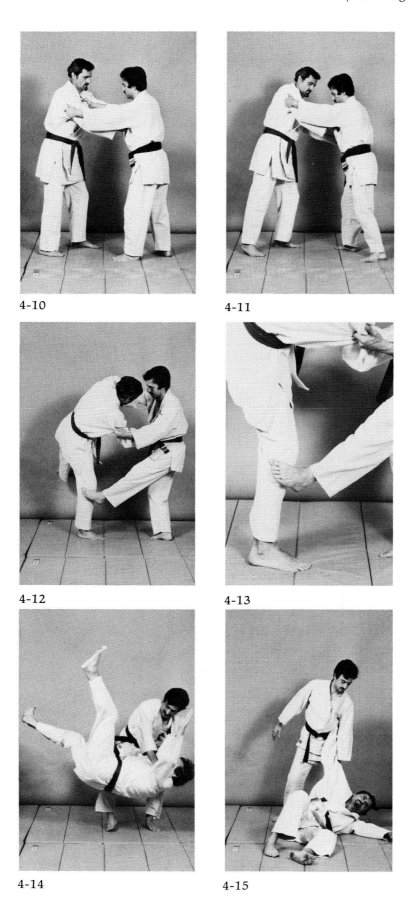

4-10

4-11

4-12

4-13

4-14

4-15

Defenses

See *Sasae Tsuri-komi Ashi* (below).

3. Sasae Tsuri-komi Ashi

Description

This throw has been around for quite a while. Two noted *judokas* who used it effectively were Yamashita (10th-degree black belt), who in 1893 made superior use of it at the Japanese Police Ministry; and Anton Geesink (6th-degree black belt), who won Olympic fame with its use. This is a superior competitive throw.

Execution

1. *Kuzushi:* Stand together and pull your left foot back slightly **(see photo 4-16)**. Step to the rear with your right foot, forcing your opponent (left, in photos) to step forward **(see photo 4-17)** with his left foot to keep his balance.

2. *Tsukuri:* With your left arm, pull forward on the opponent's right arm while pushing his left arm to the rear with your right arm **(see photo 4-18)**. At the same time, place the sole of your foot against his right ankle **(see close-up photo 4-19)**.

3. *Kake: Sweep* his foot, at the same time twisting the body from the waist and pulling forward and to the rear with your arms until he takes to the air **(see photo 4-20)** and hits the ground **(see photo 4-21)**.

Special Hints

1. Be sure to pull with all you have with the left hand.

2. Get very close to your opponent, more so than in the *Hiza-Guruma*.

3. Advanced students slam the sweeping leg into the opponent's ankle to get more power. However, this is not necessary if you apply the proper off-balancing technique.

Defenses

Lower your *center* by dropping down on the knee of the leg to be swept **(see photo 4-22)**. Be sure to push your opponent to the rear as you lower your center.

4. Uki-goshi

Description

Dr. Kano himself invented this *koshi-waza* (hip technique) throw. The throw uses a *twisting action* over the hip instead of a *popping* action as in *ogoshi*.

Execution

1. *Kuzushi:* Stand together in basic *shizentai* postures **(see photo 4-23)**. As you (right, in photos) step forward between your opponent's legs **(see photo 4-24)**, bring your right hand up under his armpit and to his back. Your opponent will step forward to resist the rear action.

4-16   4-17   4-18   4-19

4-20

4-21

4-22

4-23

4-24

2. *Tsukuri:* As he steps forward, bring your left foot back and around (see *tai-sabaki,* Chapter 2) and brace your buttocks against his lower abdomen for support *(see photo 4-25).*

3. *Kake:* Swing your arms around powerfully, rotate your hips, and roll your opponent over *(see photo 4-26)* and down *(see photo 4-27).*

Special Hints

It is important to use a powerful twisting action, utilizing the hip action and arm action to take the opponent down. These points, combined with perfect *tai-sabaki* (body shifting), will take the man down.

Defenses

The best defense against the *Uki-goshi* is to leap *(see photo 4-28)* over the leg as the twisting begins *(see photo 4-29)* and take advantage of the opponent's loss of balance by preparing to throw him to the rear *(see photo 4-30).*

5. Osoto Gari

Description

This is a very powerful leg throw (*ashi-waza*) that is very popular in competition and extremely effective when self-defense is needed.

Execution: Type 1

1. *Kuzushi:* Step to the opponent's (left, in photo) rear by placing your left foot outside and behind the opponent's right foot *(see photos 4-31, 4-32).* At the same time, pull down and behind with the left arm, and back and behind (with a twist) with the right arm. This will force your opponent off balance, up on one leg, and put him at your mercy.

2. *Tsukuri:* Place your body close to your opponent and bring your right leg up into the air *(see photo 4-33).*

3. *Kake:* Slam calf to calf *(see close-up photo 4-34),* knocking your opponent up in the air *(see photo 4-35)* and to the ground *(see photo 4-36).*

4-25

4-26

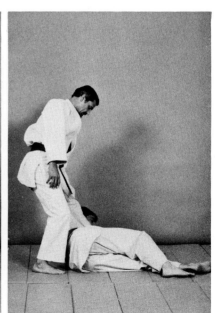

4-27

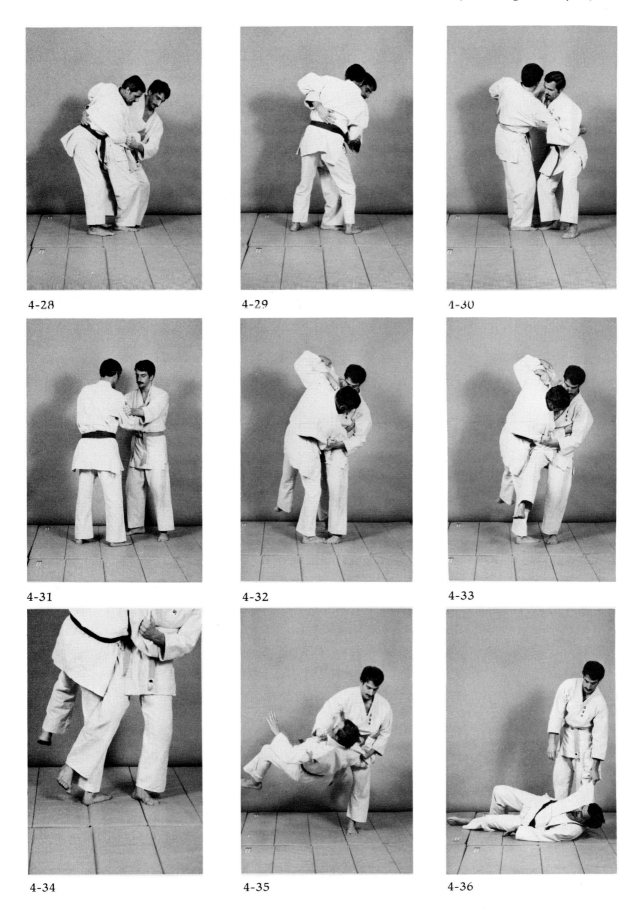

4-28

4-29

4-30

4-31

4-32

4-33

4-34

4-35

4-36

Execution: Type 2

1. *Kuzushi:* See Type 1.
2. *Tsukuri:* Instead of placing the leg calf to calf, place your lower leg against the side of your opponent's leg under the knee *(see photos 4-37, 4-38).*
3. *Kake:* The action is the same as for Type 1, except this variation puts the man a little higher in the air *(see photos 4-39, 4-40).*

Special Hints

Complete coordination is the key to executing this throw correctly. Everything must be together, not separate.

Defenses

As opponent attempts *Osoto Gari (see photo 4-41)*, resist his twisting actions and reverse the twist against him *(see photo 4-42)*. Lift the opponent's leg *(see photo 4-43)* and take him to the ground *(see photo 4-44)*.

6. Ogoshi

Description

This is a throw from the *koshi-waza* (hip category) that throws your opponent over the hip with a powerful *popping* action.

Execution

1. *Kuzushi:* You (right, in photos) and your opponent are in *jigotai* (defensive) positions *(see photo 4-45)*. Step forward with the right foot, pushing hard against the opponent *(see photo 4-46)*. He will have to push forward hard to keep his balance.
2. *Tsukiri:* As your opponent resists, pivot in by swinging the left foot to the rear counterclockwise, slamming your hip into your opponent's lower abdomen, and bending the knees *(see photo 4-47)*.
3. *Kake:* Spring up on the knees, pulling forward with the left arm and around with the right arm, which is secured around the opponent's hip *(see photo 4-48)*. The opponent will take to the air, and you will have tremendous control over him until the moment he touches the ground *(see photo 4-49)*.

Special Hints

Be sure to get your opponent to commit himself to a forward action so the hip acts as an obstruction to his forward action and he falls over. To help him fall over, be sure to bend from the knees and *pop* up.

4-37   4-38   4-39   4-40

4-41   4-42   4-43   4-44

4-45   4-46

4-47   4-48   4-49

Defenses

The best defense is to get your arm free and prevent your opponent from bending down on his knees *(see photo 4-50)*. If you can't get your arm free, you can still prevent the throw by preventing the opponent from making close body contact. This can be done by simply placing your hand on your opponent's hip and pushing away *(see photo 4-51)*.

7. Ouchi Gari

Description

This leg throw *(ashi-waza)* can be performed when either all or little of the supporting weight is on the leg to be swept. I have done it successfully both ways in competition. I find it is particularly useful for those with long, powerful legs because they can reach in and get their opponents' legs.

Execution

1. *Kuzushi:* This can be done from any posture, but the photos illustrate the natural *(shizentai)* positions *(see photo 4-52)*. Step to your opponent's (left, in photos) rear with your left leg, at the same time pushing back and pulling down very sharply with the left hand. This will force all the weight onto your opponent's right foot so you can sweep his left *(see photo 4-53)*.

2. *Tsukuri:* Reach in between the opponent's legs with your right leg and hook his left leg *(see photo 4-54)*. When you hook, be sure to do it tightly and close to prevent your opponent from slipping out *(see close-up photo 4-55)*.

3. *Kake:* Lift up the right leg, at the same time tugging down with the left arm and back, around, and down with the right arm. This will do one of two things: (1) it will throw the opponent straight back; or (2) if you are twisting powerfully, it will throw both his feet off the ground *(see photo 4-56)*. Be sure to keep a good grip on your opponent when he hits the ground so he can't get away *(see photo 4-57)*.

Special Hints

To add more power, be sure to lower your hips and drop with your knee as you twist.

4-50

4-51

4-52

4-53

4-54

4-55

4-56

4-57

8. Seoinage

Description

This throw has several variations: *Morote Seoinage* (Back-Carry Throw), *Ippon Seoinage* (One-Arm Back Carry Throw), *Kuzure Ippon Seoinage* (Trapped Arm Back Carry Throw), and *Seoi-otoshi* (Back Drop Throw). The *Seoinage* and the *Tomoe-nage* are the two most important throws in judo.

Execution: *Morote Seoinage*

1. *Kuzushi:* You (right, in photos) and your opponent are in *shizentai* position *(see photo 4-58).* Pull your opponent off balance to the right front by taking two or three *tsugi-ashi* steps to the rear.

2. *Tsukuri:* Step forward with your right foot and back-pivot with the left foot *(see photo 4-59).* Get good and close to your opponent.

3. *Kake:* Lower your center by lowering your knees and place your right elbow under your opponent's right armpit *(see photo 4-60).* Bend down and pop up, pulling the opponent over the back *(see photo 4-61).* Retain a grip on him till he reaches the mat *(see photo 4-62).*

Execution: *Ippon Seoinage*

All steps are the same as for *Morote*, except you grasp your opponent's right arm in the bend of your right arm (the right hand can also grasp the upper part of your opponent's sleeve). *(See photo 4-63).*

Execution: *Kuzure Ippon Seoinage*

1. *Kuzushi:* See *Morote Seoinage*.

2. *Tsukuri:* As you pivot in, bring the opponent's left arm around and trap it under his right armpit; the closeness of your body will keep the trapped arm secure *(see photo 4-64).*

3. *Kake:* Once trapped, follow the throwing instructions for *Morote Seoinage (see photo 4-65).*

Special Hints

In *Morote Seoinage,* as you turn, be sure that the wrist of your right hand turns inward naturally. *Do not* try to force the elbow into his right armpit.

Alternate Throws

The best alternate throw for any of the *Seoinage* throws is the *Seoi-otoshi.* However, the *Seoi-otoshi* works best as a follow-up technique for the *Ippon Seoinage.*

1. As you unsuccessfully attempt an *Ippon Seoinage,* drop down to your left knee, pulling hard to take the opponent with you *(see photo 4-66).*

2. The dropping motion will cause the opponent to fly over your back *(see photo 4-67).*

4-58

4-59

4-60

4-61

4-62

4-63

4

4-65

4-66

4-67

Set 2: *DAI NI KYO NO WAZA*
1. Ko Soto Gari

Description

With this technique the foot forms a *scoop* that takes the opponent's ankle in a clipping action. There are two types of clipping actions for this throw: (1) pulling clip, where the opponent's foot is pulled in the directions of his toes; and (2) raising clip, where the sole of the foot clips the opponent's and raises it off the floor.

Execution:

1. *Kuzushi:* Face the opponent (left, in photos) in *shizentai* posture *(see photo 4-68)*. Take a few *tsugi-ashi* steps to the rear *(see photo 4-69)*, until your opponent makes a big step forward *(see photo 4-70)*.

2. *Tsukuri:* Pivot to the side, at the same time pulling the opponent's right arm and pushing around and down with your right hand *(see photo 4-71)*.

3. *Kake:* Clip the opponent's right ankle *(see close-up photo 4-72)*, first in a pulling clip, and then turn it into a raising clip *(see photo 4-73)* to take the opponent down *(see photo 4-74)*.

Special Hints

Be sure not to relax the pulling action and the circling action of the arms on the opponent until he is down on the mat.

2. Ko Uchi Gari

Description

A very tricky and effective *ashi-waza* (leg-throwing) technique, this throw uses the same clipping actions as *Ko Soto Gari*.

Execution

1. *Kuzushi:* Stand in the *shizentai* position, facing your opponent *(see photo 4-75)*. Take a few *tsugi-ashi* steps to the rear until your opponent (left in photos) commits himself to a large step forward *(see photo 4-76)*.

2. *Tsukuri:* Pull down on your opponent's right arm (and slightly toward you) and push hard up and back with the left arm. The pushing action can either be done straight back or at an angle, catching the opponent's neck on his *kubi*, or collar *(see close-up photo 4-77)*.

3. *Kake:* At the moment you begin pushing, catch the opponent's right ankle *(see photo 4-78)* and clip it first with a pulling action and then with a raising action *(see close-up photo 4-79)*. The opponent will lose his balance *(see photo 4-80)* and fall to the rear *(see photo 4-81)*.

Special Hints

It is essential to pull the opponent's right arm down and keep it under *your* control with a *slight* pulling action toward you.

4-68

4-69

4-70

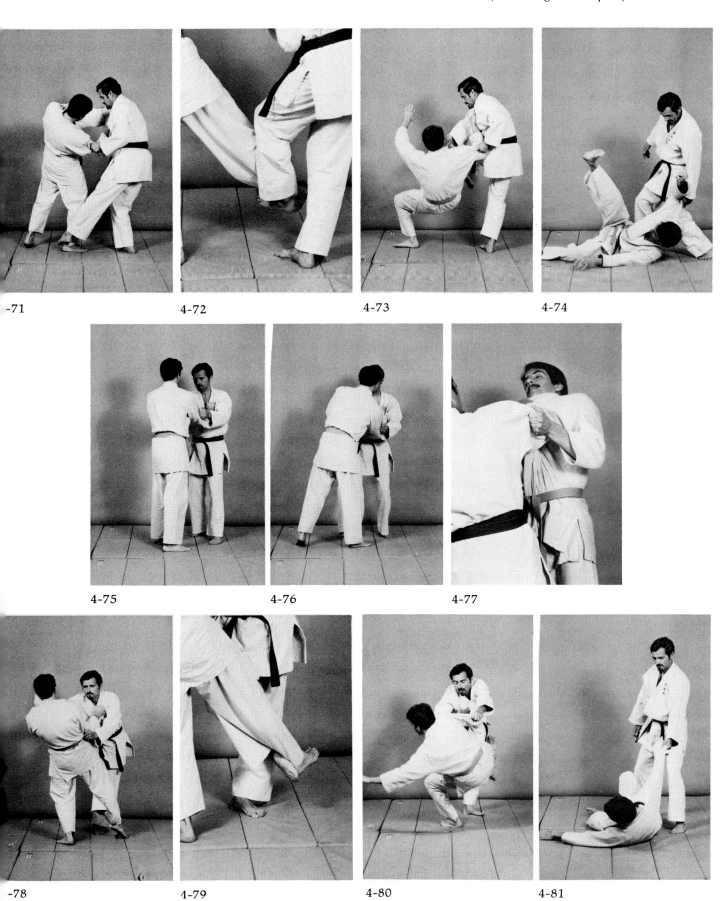

-71

4-72

4-73

4-74

4-75

4-76

4-77

-78

4-79

4-80

4-81

3. Koshi Guruma
Description

This is a *koshi-waza* (hip-throwing) technique that entraps the opponent's neck for adding take-down power.

Execution

1. *Kuzushi:* Face each other in *shizentai* position *(see photo 4-82)*. Step back hard with the left foot, forcing the opponent to step forward with his right foot.
2. *Tsukuri:* Pivot in close to your opponent *(see photo 4-83)* and at the same time begin to entrap the opponent's neck in an arm lock *(see close-up photo 4-84)*. Keep a tight grip so your opponent is locked in tight *(see close-up photo 4-85)*.
3. *Kake:* Bend on the knees and pop up, at the same time pulling your opponent by the neck *(see photo 4-86)*. This will in effect send him over your hip and to the ground *(see photo 4-87)*.

4. Tsuri Komi-goshi
Description

This throw was invented by Dr. Kano as an alternate throw for the *harai-goshi* (sweeping hip throw).

Execution

1. *Kuzushi:* Both face each other in *shizentai* posture *(see photo 4-88)*. The throw requires a great forward commitment by the opponent (left, in photos), so it is necessary to push him backward hard, forcing him to push forward.
2. *Tsukuri:* When the opponent does so, pivot in fast *(see photo 4-89)*, staying very low. The hands retain the same grip on the uniform as before to aid in the speed *(see close-up photo 4-90)*.
3. *Kake:* Bend down very low and pop up *(see photo 4-91)*, taking the opponent over the hip *(see photo 4-92)*.

Special Hints

The key to this technique is *speed*. You are essentially forcing the opponent to commit himself to a strong forward motion, and your hip acts as an obstruction over which he falls. Remember to *pop* from the hip.

4-82

4-83

4-84

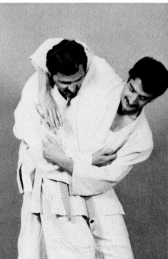

4-85

4-86

4-87

4-88

4-89

4-90

4-91

4-92

4-93

5. Okuri Ashi Harai

Description

This is a powerful but very difficult technique, where the opponent's feet are swept from the mat.

Execution

1. *Kuzushi:* In order to execute this technique, you have to break the opponent's balance from the side. Stand in *shizentai* posture *(see photo 4-94).* Step hard and fast to the left side with your left foot. The opponent (left, in photos) will have to follow and step to keep his balance *(see photo 4-95).*

2. *Tsukuri:* Leap to the right and draw your ankle up, preparing to sweep *(see photo 4-96).*

3. *Kake:* Make contact with the opponent's ankle and draw it across the floor *(see photo 4-97).* The ankles should touch *(see close-up photo 4-98).* The ankles will literally slam together, throwing the opponent *(see photo 4-99)* off his feet *(see photo 4-100).*

Special Hints

1. Be sure to leap to the side in order to gain enough momentum to throw the ankles off the mat.

2. Be sure the ankles come together.

6. Tai-otoshi

Description

This is an excellent throw for competition since it can be done over and over again if your initial effort fails. It is a very effective throw for the small person to use to defeat the large.

Execution

1. *Kuzushi:* Pull the opponent (left, in photos) back hard from *shizentai* position *(see photo 4-101).* The opponent will commit himself to a forward motion; when he does, begin the three-step pivot.

2. *Tsukuri:* For the three-step pivot, step forward with the right leg *(see photo 4-102),* pivot-step to the rear with the left leg *(see photo 4-103),* and position-step with the left leg behind the opponent's legs *(see photo 4-104).* Be sure to stay on your toes with the leg deep behind your opponent's legs.

3. *Kake:* Pull forward with the left arm, pull forward and down with the right arm, and straighten the leg all at the same instant *(see photo 4-105).* This will take your opponent down quickly *(see photo 4-106).*

Special Hints

Be sure to stay on your toes with the nonsupporting leg and pop your opponent off his feet.

4-94   4-95   4-96

4-97

4-98

4-99

4-100

4-101

4-102

4-103

4-104

4-105

4-106

4-107   4-108   4-109

Alternate Throws

The best alternate throw for the *Tai-otoshi* is the *Tai-otoshi.* Simply re-extend your leg until it works.

Defenses

Again, the best defense against the *Tai-otoshi* is itself. Leap over the opponent's throwing leg *(see photo 4-107)*, back-pivot *(see photo 4-108)*, and position in for the *Tai-otoshi (see photo 4-109).*

7. Harai-goshi

Description

Dr. Kano invented the *Harai-goshi* (sweeping hip throw). He did so to counter Shiro Saigo (a strong *jujutsuka*) and his very powerful *Uki-goshi.* The lifting action of the leg took Saigo down immediately.

Execution

1. *Kuzushi:* From a *shizentai* position *(see photo 4-110)*, step back with the left leg, drawing the opponent's (left, in photos) right foot forward *(see photo 4-111).*
2. *Tsukuri:* Skip-pivot with a leap *(see photo 4-112)*, bringing your right leg up and ready to sweep *(see photo 4-113).* Keeping in mind that this is a *koshi-waza* (hip-throwing) technique and not a leg-sweeping technique, be sure to use the entire leg and hip in positioning *(see close-up photo 4-114).*
3. *Kake:* Sweep the leg and hip up, taking the opponent's body into the air *(see photo 4-115)* and to the ground *(see photo 4-116).*

Alternate Throws

The best alternate is the *Osoto Gari,* using the same leg you attempted the *Harai-goshi* with. If the initial *Harai-goshi* fails, the opponent will have had to resist to the rear, and the *Osoto Gari* will take him down effortlessly.

Defenses

Defense 1: Kuchiki-taoshi (Dead Tree Dropping Throw). As your opponent attempts *Harai-goshi,* grab the sweeping leg *(see photo 4-117)*, and sweep the opponent's supporting ankle *(see photo 4-118)* high into the air *(see photo 4-119).*

Defense 2: Again, grab the opponent's sweeping leg *(see photo 4-120)*, but instead of sweeping him to the side as you do with the *Kuchiki-taoshi,* sweep the opponent's leg to the rear, *(see photo 4-121)* bringing his face to the mat *(see photo 4-122).*

Note: Hold the opponent by the back of the neck to keep control of him once he is down.

4-110

4-111

4-112

4-113

4-114

4-115

4-116

4-117

4-118

4-119

4-120

4-121

4-122

8. Uchi Mata

Description

This throw has been classified as both a leg and a hip technique. This author prefers the *ashi-waza* (leg-throwing) classification. I made excellent use of this throw in the open weight division at the 1974 East Coast Championships.

Execution

1. *Kuzushi:* You are facing each other in a *shizentai* position, and the opponent (left, in photos) steps toward you with his right foot and tries an attack that fails. He withdraws his foot and stands firm to resist you if you should attempt anything *(see photo 4-123)*.

2. *Tsukuri:* Pulling with both hands, force your opponent off balance to the right front *(see photo 4-124)*.

3. *Kake:* Pivot in and thrust your right leg, heel first, between your opponent's legs. Ride his thigh on your hips *(see photo 4-125)*. Using hip and leg action, sweep your opponent off his feet *(see photo 4-126)*.

Special Note: By hooking your opponent's inner leg *(see close-up photo 4-127)*, you can roll him to the ground (using the same action described above) instead of popping him off his feet.

Special Hints

Be sure to thrust your leg in deep to avoid hurting your opponent's groin.

SET 1: *DAI SAN KYO NO WAZA*

1. Ko Soto Gake

Description

This technique was conceived by Hidekazu Nagaoka, a tenth-degree black belt who began his judo training in 1915. Nagaoka was a student of *kito-ryu jujutsu* prior to studying *kodokan* judo.

When he observed the training at the *kodokan,* he saw that anytime a *judoka* would move, he would have to place the weight of the body on one leg for a moment. Nagaoka conceived the idea of hooking and knocking out the leg with the supporting weight—the theory behind the *Ko Soto Gake,* or the small outside hooking throw.

Execution

The right moment for this throw is when the opponent (left, in photos) has tensed his body and is leaning backward with his weight on one of the heels. It can be executed against an advanced or a withdrawn foot. It can also be executed against an opponent who has not advanced, and you must make him commit his weight to one leg over the other. It is with this in mind that I have selected the following photographs.

1. *Kuzushi:* Opponent is in a *shizentai* posture and is not advancing or withdrawing. Push up and to the left with the right hand and down and to the left with the left hand *(see photo 4-128)* until your opponent commits his weight to one leg *(see photo 4-129)*.

2. *Tsukuri:* Hook your opponent's outside leg *(see close-up photo 4-130)*.

3. *Kake:* Sweep the opponent's foot to your left rear, at the same time pulling down with both hands *(see photo 4-131)*. This will, if done correctly, take both of your opponent's feet into the air.

2. Tsuri-goshi

Description

This hip throw differs from the others in that there is a lifting action of the body over the hip, using the *obi* (belt). There are two types of *Tsuri-goshi:* (1) *Ko Tsuri-goshi* (minor lifting hip throw), in which the opponent's belt is grabbed under his arm; and (2) *Otsuri-goshi* (major lifting hip throw), in which you reach around *over* the opponent's shoulder and grab the belt. The *Ko Tsuri-goshi* is illustrated in this sequence.

Execution

1. *Kuzushi:* This throw is done in response

4-123

4-124

4-125

4-126

4-127

4-128

4-129

4-130

4-131

4-132

to your opponent's effort to regain his stability. From a *shizentai* posture *(see photo 4-133)* you (black belt, in photos) step to the rear, drawing your opponent's weight forward. Many times an opponent will try to regain his stability by stepping forward instead on his left foot (rather than on the right foot you are trying for). This technique can handle both responses with its pulling action *(see photo 4-134)*.

2. *Tsukuri:* Bring your right foot inside his right foot and pivot around to the rear with the left foot *(see photo 4-135)*.

3. *Kake:* Keep your hips and back tight to your opponent and grasp his belt *(see close-up photo 4-136)*. Bend on the knees slightly, pop up, and lift opponent over your hip *(see photo 4-137)* and to the ground *(see photo 4-138)*.

Special Hints

The popping and lifting actions are essential to the throwing action. Be sure to stay close to your opponent.

3. Yoko-otoshi

Description

This throw uses a throwing action to the side. It is used when the *uki-waza* throw (which uses a rear pulling action to throw the opponent to the side or rear) fails. This throw can be executed from either a *shizentai* or a *jigotai* position.

Execution

1. *Kuzushi:* Beginning from a *shizentai* position *(see photo 4-139)*, you begin to fall to the ground and pull to the rear *(see photo 4-140)*.

2. *Tsukuri:* Your opponent will resist the rear pull by stepping strongly to the side.

3. *Kake:* When he does so, fall to the ground and pull him to the side, *(see photo 4-141)* taking him to the ground *(see photo 4-142)*.

Special Hints

Be sure to fall and pull to the side at the same time to coordinate effort and maximize force.

4-133

4-134

4-135

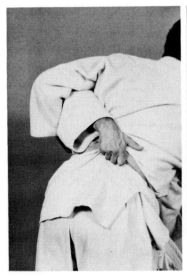

4-136

4-137

4-138

4-139

4-140

4-141

4-142

4. Ashi Guruma

Description

This throw is a personal favorite of mine. Although it may first look like a *Harai-goshi* (in fact, comparison of the *kake* photos will prove this), the actual *tsukuri* is vastly different.

Execution

1. *Kuzushi:* Start from a *shizentai* position *(see photo 4-143)*. Beginning on the left foot, take two *tsugi-ashi* steps to the rear, and draw your opponent (left, in photos) along with you. When he is about to put his advancing right foot to the floor, pull fast and hard with your left hand.

2. *Tsukuri:* The opponent will bring his right foot to his left, lean his upper body to his right front, halt his advanced foot, and lean straight over like a rod *(see photo 4-144)*.

3. *Kake:* Pull your left hand, pivot on your left toes, and put the foot's outside edge on your opponent's leg *(see photo 4-145)*. The foot must be placed below the knee *(see close-up photo 4-146)*. Apply an upward kneading action to your opponent's knee and pull hard *(see photo 4-147)* to take your opponent down *(see photo 4-148)*.

Special Hints

Be sure the pulling and pushing action of the hands and feet are in perfect harmony.

Alternate Throws

If your attempted *Ashi Guruma* fails, immediately apply a *Harai-goshi* to throw your opponent.

5. Hane-goshi

Description

This throw is believed to have been perfected by Yoshiaki Yamashita, who in 1902 taught judo to President Theodore Roosevelt. Yamashita had occasionally suffered pains in his right knee, so he favored the bent position used in this throw.

Execution

1. *Kuzushi:* From a *shizentai* posture *(see photo 4-149)*, push hard and fast while advancing on your opponent (light colored belt, in photos). He will think you are trying to throw him to the rear, and he will resist with a strong forward motion.

2. *Tsukuri:* As he pulls forward, begin to pivot *(see photo 4-150)*, and leap to your opponent's legs *(see photo 4-151)*, meeting his force head on. Place the outside of your bent leg on the inside (right below the knee) of your opponent's right leg *(see photo 4-152)*.

3. *Kake:* Bend the supporting leg slightly and stay close to your opponent *(see close-up photo 4-153)*. With a coordinated movement, raise the supporting leg and spring-kick the opponent's feet right out from under him *(see photo 4-154)*, taking him to the ground *(see photo 4-155)*.

Special Hints

The complete throwing movements must be coordinated fast, since the two of you crash head-on earlier in the throw's dynamics. Properly executed, the opponent will literally fly over you with very little effort.

4-143   4-144

4-145   4-146   4-147   4-148

4-149   4-150   4-151   4-152

4-153   4-154   4-155

6. Harai Tsuri Komi Ashi

Description

Similar in appearance to the *Sasae Tsuri-komi Ashi*, this throw uses the same *kuzushi* action but uses a quick, instantaneous sweep.

Execution

1. *Kuzushi:* Stand in *shizentai* position *(see photo 4-156)*. Force your opponent (left, in photos) off balance to his left front by pulling with both hands. Lower your upper body slightly. Your opponent will take advantage of this by resisting and stepping back on his right foot to pull you forward.

2. *Tsukuri:* At that instant, relax the pull on your right arm and put your right foot close to his feet *(see photo 4-157)*. Sweep upward into your opponent's right instep with the sole of the left foot *(see close-up photo 4-158)*.

3. *Kake:* Sweep to the rear and twist the upper and mid-body to take your opponent off his feet *(see photo 4-159)* and to the ground *(see photo 4-160)*.

Special Hints

Be sure to sweep with the hip as well as with the foot and leg. Be sure to twist with the upper and mid-body to add more power to the throw.

7. Tomoe Nage

Description

One of the most important techniques in judo, this throw truly illustrates the advantage the small man has over a larger opponent.

Execution

1. *Kuzushi:* From either a *shizentai* or a *jigotai* posture *(see photo 4-161)*, push hard against your opponent (light-colored belt in photos), forcing him to resist by pushing hard against you. When he does so, relax your pushing.

2. *Tsukuri:* Immediately coordinate his resistance and fall to the rear, placing your foot in your opponent's stomach *(see photo 4-162)*.

3. *Kake:* As you fall *(see photo 4-163)*, lift your opponent on your leg *(see photo 4-164)* and throw him to the rear or side *(see photo 4-165)*.

Special Hints

When you fall to the ground, be sure to pull both hands just above your face as if you were pulling them to the back of your head and then bring your hands down sharply at the wrists so that they end up at the sides of your ears.

4-156   4-157   4-158

4-159

4-160

4-161

4-162

4-163

4-164

4-165

8. Kata Guruma

Description

Kano invented this technique when he was a student of *tenshin-shinyo-ryu*. He was always unable to throw a certain Fukushima, a very large and well-built man. Kano studied many books on *sumo* and *jujutsu* and came up with this technique, which took Fukushima into the air and crashing to the ground.

Execution

1. *Kuzushi:* From a *shizentai* posture *(see photo 4-166)*, force your opponent (light-colored belt, in photos) to open his legs (if they are open, fine; if they are not, try an *Ouchi Gari* leg sweep to force them apart). When your opponent's legs are apart, force him off balance by pulling him hard with your left hand to his right front.

2. *Tsukuri:* Step in between your opponent's legs with your right leg *(see photo 4-167)*, keeping a grip on his sleeve with your left hand and grabbing his inner right leg with your right hand.

3. *Kake:* Lift your opponent on your shoulders with knees bent, or even the right knee on the mat *(see photo 4-168)*. Stand erect, pulling down with the left arm and up and over with the right arm *(see photo 4-169)*, taking your opponent over and down *(see photo 4-170)*.

Combat-Efficient Variation

This has the same *kuzushi* as the standard version, but throw yourself at your opponent's legs *(see photo 4-171)*, staying in a kneeling position *(see photo 4-172)*, and dump your opponent over your shoulders *(see photo 4-173)*.

Special Hints

Be sure to get the opponent moving toward you so he himself helps you with the lifting action, or else he may be too heavy for you.

4-166

4-167

4-168

4-169

4-170

4-171

4-172

4-173

SET 4: *DAI YON KYO NO WAZA*

1. Sumi Gaeshi

Description

This technique is very similar to *Tomae Nage*, except this throw dumps your opponent to your side.

Execution

1. *Kuzushi:* From a *jigotai* posture *(see photo 4-174)*, force your opponent (light colored belt, in photos) to resist and lead his energy forward. When he does so, push hard on his left sleeve, drawing his weight onto his right foot.

2. *Tsukuri:* Fall to your rear *(see photo 4-175)*, placing the instep of your left foot into his inner left thigh *(see close-up photo 4-176)*.

3. *Kake:* Pull down with your left hand, up and over with your right hand, and up and to the side with your left leg *(see photo 4-177)*, throwing your opponent to your side *(see photo 4-178)*.

Special Hints

Be sure to slide your left foot between his legs as you force him off balance.

Alternate Throws

Follow up with a *Yoko-otoshi* or *Uki-waza*, if the *Sumi Gaeshi* should fail you.

2. Tani-otoshi

Description

This is a very effective throw with which to counter an opponent who constantly stands in a defensive posture. Translated as the "valley drop throw," it is best applied when the opponent has placed all his weight on his heels.

Execution

1. *Kuzushi:* From the *jigotai* position *(see photo 4-179)*, pull firmly and straight down to your opponent's (left, in photos) heels on his right sleeve.

2. *Tsukuri:* Place your left leg behind your opponent's legs *(see photo 4-180)*.

3. *Kake:* Drop to the floor, pulling straight down with the left hand and back and down with the right hand *(see photo 4-181)*. This will take your opponent down to his back *(see photo 4-182)*.

Special Hints

Be prepared for *ne-waza* techniques after you have taken the opponent down.

3. Hane Maki-komi

Description

This is a throw in which you sacrifice your own balance to take the opponent down.

4-174

4-175

4-176

4-177

4-178

4-179

4-180

4-181

4-182

Execution

1. *Kuzushi:* From a *jigotai* posture *(see photo 4-183)*, prevent the opponent (light-colored belt, in photos) from grabbing you in Grip C. This is accomplished at the onset of the match, before you have grabbed each other. You can prevent this by grabbing his left wrist from the inside with your right hand. Take a couple of *tsugi-ashi* steps to the rear, beginning with your left foot. As you do so, bring your left arm around as if you were going to put it on the left side of your head and raise your opponent, drawing him off balance to the front right *(see photo 4-184)*.

2. *Tsukuri:* The opponent will follow you as you lead and will begin to put his left foot down on the mat. When he does so, pivot in, wrapping his arm securely around your side, *(see photo 4-185)* and place your foot in a bent position inside your opponent's right leg (see *Hane-goshi* for details of spring leg action) *(see photo 4-186)*.

3. *Kake:* Kick his feet out from the mat and throw your body to your right side *(see photo 4-187)*, taking your opponent down with you *(see photo 4-188)*.

4. Sukui Nage

Description

The throw gets its name from the "scoop-ing" action (*sukui*) of the opponent's body (light-colored belt, in photos). This throw requires a great deal of speed to take the opponent by surprise.

Execution

1. *Kuzushi:* From *shizentai* position *(see photo 4-189)*, pull the opponent forward. He resists by stepping back on his right foot.

2. *Tsukuri:* Step to his left side from behind (using a back pivot), placing your right leg behind your opponent and wrapping your arms on his waist *(see photo 4-190)*.

3. *Kake:* Lift your opponent up behind his thighs with a scooping motion, twisting him to your left *(see photo 4-191)*, and throwing him behind you *(see photo 4-192)*.

Special Hints

For more power, swing your pelvic region up and out, at the same time scooping your opponent with your arms in an upward, rear-scooping action.

Defenses

Wrap your leg around your opponent's leg to prevent him from scooping you *(see photo 4-193)*.

4-183

4-184

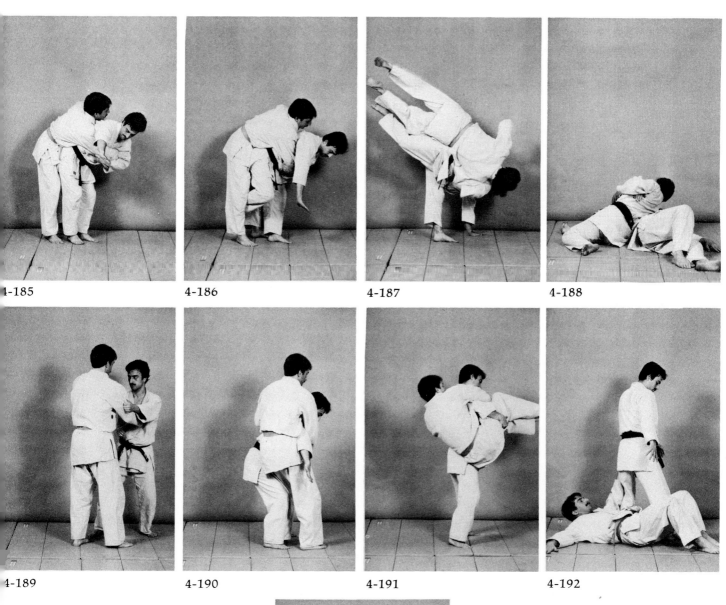

4-185   4-186   4-187   4-188

4-189   4-190   4-191   4-192

4-193

5. Utsuri-goshi

Description

An extremely difficult throw to execute under real conditions, the *Utsuri-goshi*, or changing hip throw, is used to counter techniques such as *Ippon Seoinage, Uchi Mata,* or *Harai-goshi*. During the countering action, one executes an *Ushiro-goshi* and changes it then to an *Ogoshi;* thus the term *changing hip throw.*

Execution

1. *Kuzushi:* You stand in *shizentai* position *(see photo 4-194),* and your opponent (light-colored belt, in photos) attempts an *Ippon Seoinage (see photo 4-195).*
2. *Tsukuri:* Wrap your left arm around your opponent's waist while your right hand grabs your opponent's right sleeve (or under his thigh for shorter/smaller individuals). Thrust your hips forward and upward and lift your opponent off his feet *(see photo 4-196).*
3. *Kake:* As your opponent comes down again, using both hands and a twisting action of your left hip to right, switch the opponent's body onto your left hip *(see photo 4-197),* executing an *Ogoshi* throw *(see photo 4-198)* to take your opponent down *(see photo 4-199).*

Special Hints

This throw requires more timing and speed than it does power. I have proven this time and again in open weight competition. The idea is to switch from one hip to the next smoothly with speed and unbroken rhythm.

6. O-guruma

Description

Looking very much like the *Harai-goshi,* the *O-guruma* (major wheel) uses only the action of the legs, making it a *ashi-waza* technique.

Execution

The time to execute this throw is when the opponent (light-colored belt, in photos) comes to the right front position.

1. *Kuzushi:* From a *shizentai* posture *(see photo 4-200),* pull hard with the left hand to force your opponent to step forward on the right foot to the right front *(see photo 4-201).*
2. *Tsukuri:* Place the ball of the left foot on the mat in front of your own right foot and pivot on the ball in a counterclockwise movement, putting the right leg to your opponent's legs *(see photo 4-202).*
3. *Kake:* Pull down and forward with your left hand and forward and down with your right hand, while lifting the leg in a sweeping action against your opponent's stationary legs *(see photo 4-203).* This will take your opponent down *(see photo 4-204).*

4-194   4-195   4-196

4-197

4-198

4-199

4-200

4-201

4-202

4-203

4-204

7. Soto Maki-komi

Description

Soto Maki-komi is executed the same as *Hane Maki-komi*, except both feet stay on the mat and do not spring out the opponent's supporting legs.

Execution

1. *Kuzushi:* From a *jigotai* posture *(see photo 4-205)*, prevent your opponent (light-colored belt, in photos) from grabbing you in a C grip. This is accomplished at the onset of the throw, before you have grabbed each other. You can prevent this by grabbing his left wrist from the inside with your right hand. Take a couple of *tsugi-ashi* steps to the rear, beginning with your left foot. As you do so, bring your left arm around as if you were going to put it on the left side of your head and raise the opponent, drawing him off balance to the front right *(see photo 4-206)*.

2. *Tsukuri:* The opponent will follow you as you lead and will begin to put his left foot down on the mat. When he does so, pivot in, wrapping his arm securely around your side *(see photo 4-207)*.

3. *Kake:* Throw your opponent by falling to the right side *(see photo 4-208)*, going down to the mat with your opponent *(see photo 4-209)*.

8. Uki-otoshi

Description

This is a very gentle throw that epitomizes the concept of *ju* (yielding).

Execution

The throw is executed when you get the opponent (left, in photos) to commit himself to a large, unstable step forward.

1. *Kuzushi:* From *shizentai* position, take several *tsugi-ashi* steps to the rear until the opponent steps forward hard with his right foot to try to regain his stability *(see photo 4-210)*.

2. *Tsukuri:* As the opponent makes that hard forward step, drop to your left knee, pulling hard to your rear in a circular motion *(see photo 4-211)* in order to pull your opponent off balance completely *(see photo 4-212)*.

3. *Kake:* The loss of balance, the pulling, and the dropping to the knee will take your opponent off his feet *(see photo 4-213)* and to the ground *(see photo 4-214)*.

Special Hints

Do not be jerky with this technique. Let all pieces fit together smoothly and rhythmically.

4-205

4-206

4-207   4-208   4-209

4-210   4-211   4-212

4-213   4-214

SET 5: *DAI GO KYO NO WAZA*

1. O Soto Guruma

Description

This is a powerful technique that clips both legs out from under your opponent.

Execution

1. *Kuzushi:* From a *shizentai* position *(see photo 4-215)*, pull forward hard with both hands, forcing your opponent (left, in photos) to resist to the rear.
2. *Tsukuri:* When he does so, slip your right leg behind your opponent *(see photo 4-216)*.
3. *Kake:* Time his resistance with your sweeping action of both supporting legs *(see photo 4-217)* to throw your opponent to the ground *(see photo 4-218)*.

Alternate Throw

If the initial *Osoto Guruma* fails, put your leg straight behind your opponent *(see photo 4-219)* and throw your entire weight against him *(see photo 4-220)* to drop him over your leg *(see photo 4-221)*. This technique is called *O-soto-otoshi.*

2. Uki Waza

Description

Like the *Uki-otoshi,* the *Uki Waza* is a true representation of the concept of *ju* (gentleness). Kazuzo Kudo (ninth-degree black belt), once said that those who can do both the left- and right-side versions of this throw correctly can call themselves true judo masters.

Execution

The time to execute this technique is when the opponent is forward and off balance to his right front outside.

It can be performed two ways: (1) lift-pull the opponent to lead him to right front; or (2) lead the opponent to the right front with a lift/pull, step to the left, and fall to the mat, taking him with you.

1. *Kuzushi:* From a *shizentai* posture *(see photo 4-222)*, pull your opponent (left, in photos) hard with the right hand *(see photo 4-223)*, at the same time stepping to the rear with the right foot. Your opponent will have to step forward on his left foot to keep his balance.
2. *Tsukuri:* Raise both hands up and to the right in a counterclockwise twist, getting closer to your opponent *(see photo 4-224)*.
3. *Kake:* Open your body to the left and step back on your left foot, forcing your opponent off balance to his right front outside. Turn your body to the left, fall back *(see photo 4-225)*, and, using both hands, throw your opponent to your left side (or rear) *(see photo 4-226)*.

4-215   4-216   4-217   4-218

4-219

4-220

4-221

4-222

4-223

4-224

4-225

4-226

3. Yoko Wakare

Description

This throw can be done in two distinct ways: (1) the way it is illustrated here; (2) the same actions of *tsukuri* and *kuzushi* are followed, but the *kake* differs. Instead of using the leg to help take the man over, the body is held straight as an arrow on the mat and the opponent flies over it. My first instructor of judo, Master Lane, felt that the first method is the most pure; therefore, I have chosen that method to illustrate.

Execution

1. *Kuzushi:* Push hard against your opponent (left, in photos) with both hands as if you were about to attempt a throw to his rear *(see photo 4-227)*. Your opponent will resist forward; as he does so, prepare to meet his energy.

2. *Tsukuri:* Swing the left leg across your opponent's path *(see photo 4-228)* in order to gain momentum (this movement is optional and is not considered a classical move in some judo circles). Throw the body up into the air *(see photo 4-229)*, and land out to the left rear, pulling hard on your opponent *(see photo 4-230)*.

3. *Kake:* As you land, you will be drawing your opponent down with you. In order to prevent him from falling on top of you, catch his feet with your right leg *(see photo 4-231)* and pull hard with both hands. The combined action of pulling, falling, and lifting his legs with yours, coupled with the fact that you meet his resisting force by yielding to it, will roll him over your body *(see photo 4-232)* and down to the mat *(see photo 4-233)*.

Special Hints

Remember, when you fall to the mat, do not fall at his feet directly but instead slightly to your rear.

4. Yoko Guruma

Description

Again, this throw, like the *Yoko Wakare*, has two distinctly different methods of execution. The first way (illustrated), gets its "wheel" (*guruma*) action from the spinning motion of the body as it evades an opponent's technique. The second way involves simply dropping down at your opponent's feet (without a spin) and pulling him over in a "wheel" action similar to the movement of the *Ura Nage*. I was very confused on which one to illustrate as the "classical way." My dear friend Dr. Yukio Okura, a professor at Tokyo University and a great martial arts historian, suggested the method illustrated.

Execution

1. *Kuzushi:* From a *shizentai* posture *(see photo 4-234)*, your opponent (right, in photos) attempts an *Ogoshi* or *Uki-goshi* (in fact, this throw can be done against a variety of throws with similar *tsukuri*) *(see photo 4-235)*. Step around the opponent's legs to avoid the throw *(see photo 4-236)*. The opponent is now in an off-balanced position.

2. *Tsukuri:* Fall to the ground *(see photo 4-237)*, pulling hard with the right hand and back and around with the left hand *(see photo 4-238)*.

3. *Kake:* This pulling and falling action, coupled with the fact that the opponent is off-balanced and taken by surprise by the counter, will take him into the air *(see photo 4-239)* and to the mat *(see photo 4-240)*.

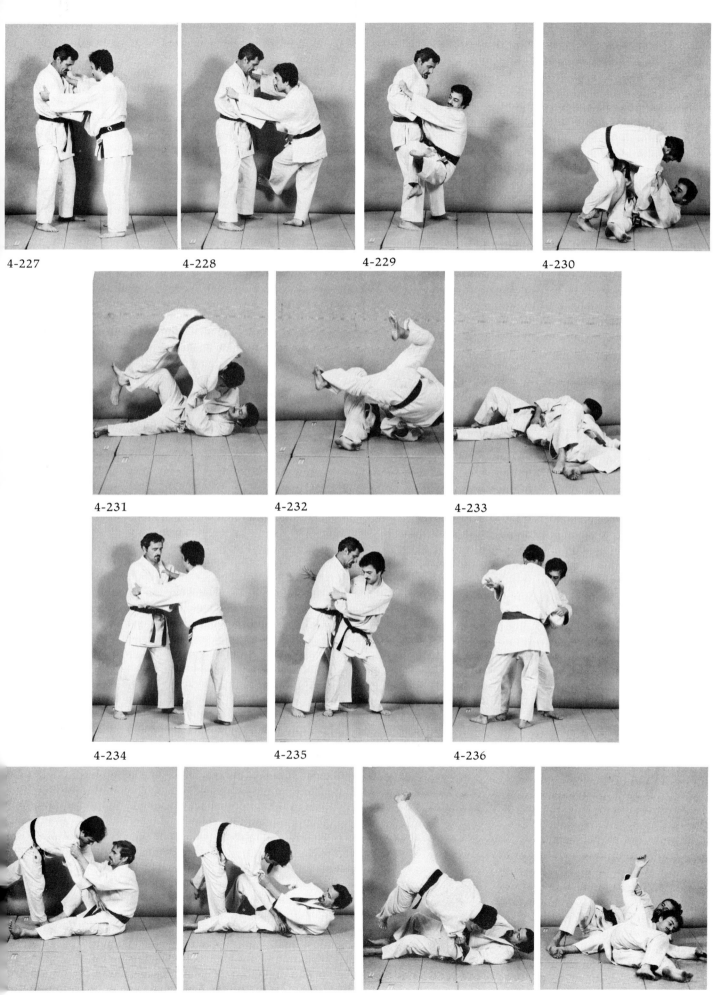

4-227

4-228

4-229

4-230

4-231

4-232

4-233

4-234

4-235

4-236

4-237

4-238

4-239

4-240

5. Ushiro-goshi

Description

Although this throw can be used offensively, it is best used as a defense against another throw.

Execution

1. *Kuzushi:* From *shizentai* posture *(see photo 4-241)*, your opponent (light-colored belt, in photos) attempts an *Ippon Seoinage (see photo 4-242)*.

2. *Tsukuri:* Lower your body to avoid the technique and wrap the right hand around his waist and the left hand under his upper left thigh (or both hands can be wrapped around his waist).

3. *Kake:* Raise your body up and thrust your hips up and out, at the same time using hand action in an upward direction *(see photo 4-243)*. This will throw your opponent *(see photo 4-244)*.

6. Ura Nage

Description

This throw is best accomplished when the opponent comes rushing at you, attempting to strike you (as is done in the judo *kata Nage-No-Kata*). This will take the opponent directly over your back. However, in general throwing for *randori* purposes, the *Ura Nage* throws the opponent to the rear.

Execution

1. *Kuzushi:* From *shizentai* posture *(see photo 4-245)*, step forward on your left foot, gripping your opponent's (left, in photos) right wrist from the inside with your left hand to get control of it and prevent him from getting a C grip on you.

2. *Tsukuri:* You can proceed in one of two ways. These are labeled for the *tori* (executor) of large or small frame. I will explain the large frame and will explain and illustrate the small frame.

Large Frame: Advance your left foot from his right side to his right rear, lower your hips, and hug him close to you. The left side of the chest will touch his body from the right hip to under his right arm. Wrap your left arm around his buttocks and put your right hand, palm down, on the right side of the lower abdomen.

Small Frame: Let go of your opponent's wrist and immediately grab him on the upper collar with your left hand and the upper inside left thigh with the right hand *(see photo 4-246)*.

3. *Kake* (same for both large and small man): Lower your hips and scoop your opponent up by bending backward. When your opponent's feet leave the mat slightly, fall backward *(see photo 4-247)*, throwing your opponent either straight back or to the upper rear side *(see photo 4-248)*.

4-241

4-242

4-243

4-244

4-245

4-246

4-247

4-248

7. Sumi-otoshi

Description

This throw takes your opponent down with body dynamics and the principle of *ju*, with *no* body contact other than the hands. That is why it is classified as a *te-waza* (hand-throwing) technique. It is sometimes called *Kuki Nage.*

Execution

1. *Kuzushi:* From a *shizentai* posture *(see photo 4-249)*, take a few *tsugi-ashi* steps to the rear *(see photo 4-250)*. When your opponent (left, in photos) follows, raise his left side with your right hand so that the left foot is slightly off the mat.

2. *Tsukuri:* Bring your right foot behind your left foot to form a *T.* When you accomplish the *T* formation (wide open) bend from the knees, lowering your hips. Move your left foot behind your opponent's right heel.

3. *Kake:* Spring up and twist counterclockwise, at the same time pulling down and straight back with the left hand and down and around with the right hand *(see photo 4-251)*, taking your opponent off his feet *(see photo 4-252)* and down to the mat *(see photo 4-253)*.

Special Hints

Be sure to coordinate the twisting action of the hips (make it strong) with the pulling, twisting, and turning actions of the hands.

8. Yoko Gake

Description

This throw is most often used as a last resort to get someone you cannot execute a clean throw on down to the mat for grappling techniques. The advantage of the throw is that it will nearly always get the man down. The disadvantage is that you yourself are also down and in a position that gives him an equal chance to get a hold on you. The solution: throw him and move in fast and accurately with *ne-waza.*

Execution

1. *Kuzushi:* From a *shizentai* position *(see photo 4-254)*, step back on the left foot, at the same time pulling your opponent's (left, in photos) right arm, forcing him to step forward with the right foot *(see photo 4-255)*.

2. *Tsukuri:* Hook your opponent's right ankle with the sole of your left foot *(see photo 4-256)*.

3. *Kake:* Sweep his leg up *(see photo 4-257)*, at the same time pulling straight down hard with the left hand and down and back hard with the right hand *(see photo 4-258)*, at the same time falling to your back. This will take your opponent and you down *(see photo 4-259)*.

4-249

4-250

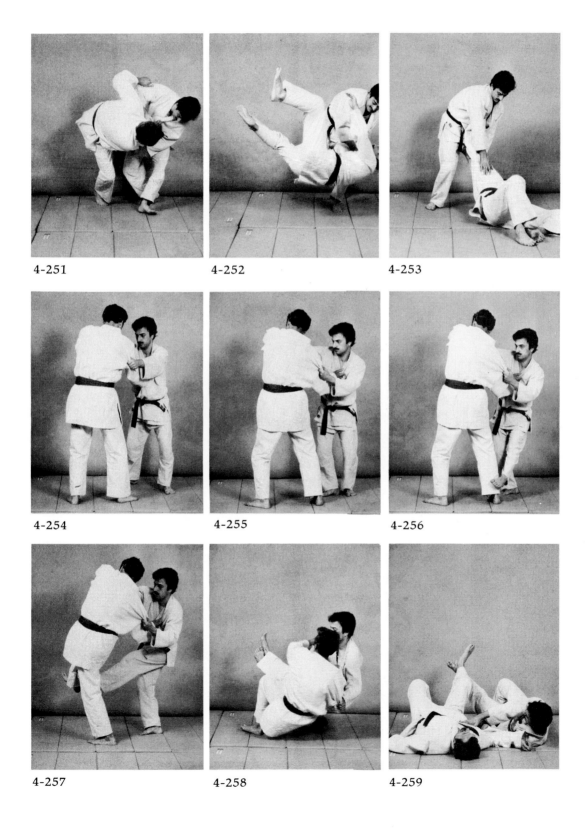

4-251   4-252   4-253

4-254   4-255   4-256

4-257   4-258   4-259

5
KATAME-WAZA
(PINNING, LOCKING, AND CHOKING TECHNIQUES)

Although most beginners think that judo is made up of only throwing techniques, *ne-waza*, or mat work, plays an intricate role (as does *atemi-waza* or striking/kicking).

Ne-waza means groundwork or mat techniques, while *katame-waza* translates roughly as grappling techniques. Both terms are used synonymously.

Katame-waza is broken down into several parts: (1) *osaekomi-waza* (pinning techniques), (2) *kansetsu-waza* (joint manipulation techniques), and (3) *shime-waza* (choking techniques).

Since *katame-waza* are (unlike throws) techniques of submission, it is wise to understand the ways one can surrender when choked or locked to avoid injury. This is done by shouting *"mai tai"* (surrender) or by slapping the mat hard twice (or your opponent twice). This will let the opponent know you have had enough and are giving up. *Do not* try to see how long you can take it. If the pain is there and the lock or choke is solid, surrender. Better to give up than to be injured.

OSAEKOMI-WAZA

Many of the holding techniques in judo resemble those of AAU wrestling. The only difference is the rules. In judo a pin does not involve holding the opponent's shoulder's on the mat for a count of three; rather, it requires that you pin his back to the mat and have complete control over him for thirty seconds. Having control means that although he can squirm, he cannot escape the hold. Pinning techniques are often performed in a slow and relaxed manner. Frantic thrashing about will work against you in judo, especially if your opponent is skilled.

Some objectives in pinning techniques:

1. Place all your weight on the center of your opponent's chest.
2. Keep your body low, close to the mat, and close to the opponent.
3. Do not leave any space between you and the opponent.
4. Hold tightly and firmly but not stiffly.
5. Be relaxed so that you can be flexible

and ready to change from one hold to another.

6. Apply your strength freely and rhythmically.

7. Use your strength in a continuous motion to control your opponent's attempts at breaking free.

8. Seek out his weak points and apply your own strengths to them.

Technique 1: *Kesa Gatame* (Scarf Hold)

Application

This technique is excellent for use when speed is essential. However, it does not have as much control over your opponent as do other holds.

1. Move in on your opponent when you are still holding his sleeve from the throw. Step in on his right side and move in very close.

2. Hold his right arm by the sleeve and secure it under your left armpit.

3. Wrap your right arm under your opponent's neck and grasp his right sleeve *(see photo 5-1)*.

4. Extend your legs as if riding a bike.

5. Place your head near your opponent's head to add more control (optional) *(see photo 5-2)*.

6. If necessary, you can place your head against your opponent's temple to add control *(see close-up photo 5-3)*.

Technique 2: *Kuzure Kesa Gatame* (Variation of Scarf Hold)

Application

Proceed as for *kesa gatame*, except your right arm goes around his back *(see photo 5-4)* instead of around his head.

Note: This technique is not as effective as the *kesa gatame* because you have less control over your opponent's left arm.

Technique 3: *Ushiro Kesa Gatame* (Rear Scarf Hold)

Application

1. Slide in on your opponent's right side.

2. Pin your opponent's right arm with your right armpit.

3. Slip your left arm above your opponent's left shoulder and grasp his belt (*obi*) *(see photo 5-5)*.

4. Extend your legs as if you were riding a bike.

Technique 4: *Kata Gatame* (Shoulder Hold)

Application

This hold is excellent for pinning a larger opponent (especially by a smaller man).

1. Move in on your opponent's right side, retaining your grip on his right arm after throwing him.

2. Move the opponent's right arm to the side and press your right knee against his right side. Extend the left leg for stability.

3. Trap your opponent's right arm between the left side of your neck and the right side of his head and grasp your left wrist with your right hand. *(See photo 5-6, which shows close-up detail of the hand position; however, in reality, this detail shown in the photo is on the mat, hidden from sight).*

4. Control your opponent by pressing head to head *(see photo 5-7)*.

Technique 5: *Kami Shiho Gatame* (Upper Four Quarters Hold)

Application

This technique is a good follow-up to sacrificing throws or as an alternate hold-down to *kesa gatame* or *yoko shiho gatame*.

1. Move into your opponent from the direction of his head.

2. Place your body close to his with the weight on the center of your opponent's chest.

3. Wrap your arms under your opponent's shoulders, squeezing his arms close to his body (to control them) and grasping his belt *(see photo 5-8)*.

4. Bring your knees to the opponent's shoulders *(see rear detail in photo 5-9)*.

5-1

5-2

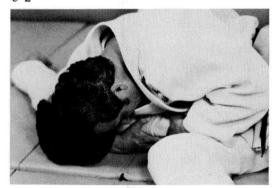

5-3

5-6

5-7

5-4

5-8

5-5

5-9

Technique 6: *Kuzure Kami Shiho Gatame 1* (Variation 1 of Four Quarters Hold)

Application

This is the same as *kami shiho gatame*, except the legs are extended outward and up on the ball of the feet. All weight bears down on the opponent's upper chest and shoulders *(see photo 5-10)*.

Technique 7: *Kuzure Kami Shiho Gatame 2* (Variation 2 of Four Quarters Hold)

Application

1. Move in on your opponent from the direction of his head.
2. Thrust your right arm under your opponent's right arm and grab his collar (you can trap his right arm under your right armpit if possible).
3. Hold your opponent's left arm close to his body with your left arm, grasping his belt *(see photo 5-11)*.
4. Bring your left knee up and extend your right leg *(see detail of left side in photo 5-12)*.

Technique 8: *Yoko Shiho Gatame* (Side Four Directions Hold)

Application

1. Attack your opponent from the side.
2. Wrap your right arm under his neck, grasping his collar.
3. Reach in between his legs with your left hand and grasp his belt.
4. Bring your knees to the opponent's side (or extend the legs on the balls of the feet).
5. Bear the weight down on your opponent's mid-chest *(see photo 5-13)*.

Technique 9: *Tate Shiho Gatame* (Vertical Four Directions Hold)

Application

This is an excellent follow-up attack (alternate hold-down) for *yoko shiho gatame*.

1. Your opponent is on his back, lying face up.
2. Straddle him, placing your weight on mid-chest.
3. Extend his right arm, holding it under control.
4. Extend his left arm, grasping him on his left collar; or pin his left arm to his side, holding it with left arm, and grasp his belt under his left waist.
5. For greater control, "grapevine" his legs to prevent him from wiggling out (optional) *(see photo 5-14)*.

Technique 10: *Kuzure Tate Shiho Gatame* (Variation on Vertical Four Directions Hold)

Application

1. This is the same as *tate shiho gatame*, but slip your right arm around the opponent's neck *(see detail of hand position in photo 5-15)*.
2. You can grasp your belt for added strength on the hold (optional) *(see photo 5-16)*.

KANSETSU-WAZA

Kansetsu-waza is the art of twisting and bending body joints to cause pain or breakage. In sport judo, only elbow locks are permitted. However, judo contains many knee and leg locks for self-defense purposes. We will explain only those techniques applicable to modern sport judo, though many of them can also be used in self-defense.

When applying joint locks, follow these tips:

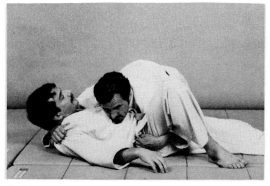

5-13

5-10

5-14

5-11

5-15

5-12

5-16

1. When applying a lock to the elbow, it must be done slowly and firmly (this will give your opponent a chance to surrender before you cause damage to the joint).
2. Never *snap* pressure on a joint in competition or you will break the joint.
3. Keep your grip firm but relaxed so, if the first lock fails, you can switch quickly to the next.

Technique 1: *Ude Garami* (Arm Wrap)

Application

1. The opponent is lying face up.
2. Move in from the right side, lying across the opponent's body with knees tucked in close to his side.
3. Bend the opponent's arm so the elbow faces downward, grasping his left wrist with your left hand.
4. Wrap your right arm under his left arm and grab your own wrist *(see photo 5-17)*.
5. Pressure is applied by wrenching your right arm upward and twisting his elbow back.

Technique 2: *Kuzure Ude Garami* (Variation of Arm Wrap)

Application

This technique is applied if you have been thrown and your opponent is coming down to grapple with you. The technique is applied with you on your back.

1. As the opponent comes in to pin you, grab the opponent's right wrist with your left hand.
2. Slip your right hand under the opponent's upper left arm. Seize your left wrist with your right hand *(see photo 5-18)*.
3. Pressure is applied by twisting the arm up and out in a clockwise direction.

Technique 3: *Ude Gatame* (Arm Crush)

Application

1. Your opponent is lying on the mat, face up.
2. Put your right knee on the mat and your left knee on the opponent's stomach (or hip).
3. Grasp his arm, turning his elbow away from you, and rest his hand on your right shoulder.
4. Put the palm of your right hand on the opponent's elbow and the palm of the left hand below right or put the left palm on the right palm.
5. Pressure is applied by pressing his elbow toward you *(see photo 5-19)*. Your knee position will prevent him from moving.

Technique 4: *Kuzure Ude Gatame* (Variation of Arm Crush)

Application

This technique is an excellent defense against an opponent who constantly applies a straight arm in standing position to prevent you from moving in on him.

1. Face each other in *shizentai* position *(see photo 5-20)*.
2. Apply the leg and *kuzushi* action of a *harai tsuri-komi-ashi*, but go down with the opponent *(see photo 5-21)*.
3. As you are going down, put your opponent's right stiff arm on your left shoulder, pressing the elbow (reversed) downward.
4. Place your right foot on your opponent's left knee and your left on opponent's right knee. This will give you control over his movements *(see photo 5-22)*.
5. Your opponent is locked into a position of nonmovement. Pressure is applied by pressing the elbow downward *(see photo 5-23)*.

5-17

5-20

5-18

5-21

5-22

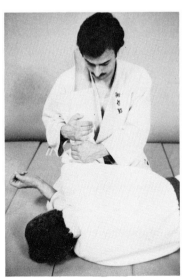

5-19

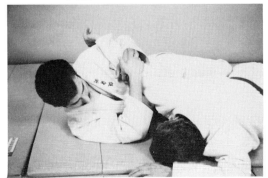

5-23

Technique 5: *Juji Gatame* Crossed-Arm Lock)

Application

This is an extremely fast technique to get into, and the pain is instantaneous for your opponent.

1. When your opponent is thrown, retain your grip on his right arm.
2. Grasp his right wrist with both hands.
3. Place your right instep under his right armpit and your left leg across his neck.
4. Fall to the mat, retaining a grip on your opponent's wrist and placing the opponent's elbow on your right inside thigh (near the groin).
5. Your legs will prevent him from rising (as will the pain).
6. Pain is applied by pulling the wrist down and at the same time raising your pelvic region upward *(see photo 5-24)*.

Technique 6: *Kuzure Juji Gatame* (Variation of Crossed-Arm Lock)

Application

This technique is used when your opponent tries to roll himself facedown to prevent you from pinning him.

1. As your opponent turns over, keep a grip on his left wrist with both hands and tuck his arm between your thighs.
2. Fall face first to the mat, retaining your grip on your opponent's arm.
3. Both your feet and legs should be across his chest, pinned to the mat.

4. Pressure is applied by pulling the arm upward against the elbow *(see photo 5-25)*.

Technique 7: *Hiza Gatame* (Knee Hold)

Application

In this hold the pressure is not applied *against* the knee, but pressure is applied against the elbow *by* the knee.

1. Both you and your opponent are on your left knees with right knees raised.
2. Clamp his left wrist under your right armpit.
3. Grasp the upper outside portion of his sleeve with your left hand. Grip the lapel of his *gi* in your right hand.
4. Bring your right foot to the front of his left thigh. Stretch your right leg out and twist to the left with your hips.
5. Bend the left leg and place it on your opponent's right lower side, bending the knee.
6. Pressure is applied by pressing downward with your bent right knee against the opponent's elbow *(see photo 5-26)*.

Technique 8: *Kuzure Hiza Gatame* (Variation of Knee Hold)

Application

Follow *hiza gatame* exactly, but instead of putting the foot on your opponent's lower side in step 5, wrap it over the opponent's arm and up and under his chin. Pressure is applied by pushing your opponent's wrist up and pressing your knee down *(see photo 5-27)*.

5-24

5-25

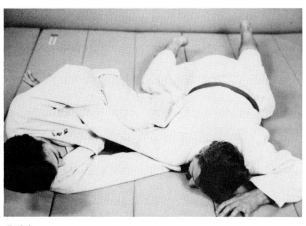

5-26

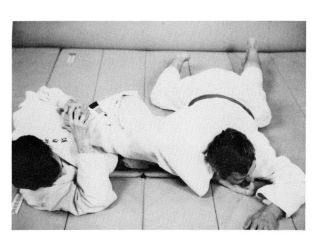

5-27

Technique 9: *Waki Gatame (Armpit Hold)*

Application

This technique is applied against an opponent who tries to evade you by sticking his buttocks out and locking his arms so you can't move in.

1. Start from a tight, resisting *jigotai* posture *(see photo 5-28)*.
2. Pull your right arm free. This can be done by circling his hand clockwise or counterclockwise and pulling out of the grip.
3. Step hard to the rear with the right leg and circle around to your opponent's right side.
4. While stepping, be sure to turn your opponent's elbow up and wrap your left arm over it, placing your opponent's upper arm in your left armpit *(see photo 5-29)*.
5. Place all your weight on your opponent's upper right shoulder, dropping down on the left knee and raising the opponent's arm skyward *(see photo 5-30)*.
6. Finish by pinning your opponent to the ground and twisting your opponent's arm clockwise, at the same time putting reverse pressure on the elbow joint *(see photo 5-31)*.

SHIME-WAZA

The choking techniques in competitive judo are not choking techniques in the sense that they cut off air by applying pressure to the windpipe or larynx. Instead, they cut off the blood supply to the head, forcing the opponent to lose consciousness for a few seconds. It takes about ten seconds for an opponent to lose consciousness once the choke is applied in full. Actually, he simply faints, coming back in a few seconds—that is, provided the pressure has stopped. Thus, it is advised that if your opponent secures a choke hold on you and you cannot break it, *surrender* before losing consciousness.

If you find yourself in a choke hold, the only defense is to turn toward the choking arm and drop chin to chest. This will relieve some of the pressure. Remember, though, if the choke is in tight, it is best to surrender.

The best ways to maintain a good choke:

1. Make sure you have complete control over your opponent and complete control over your own freedom of action.
2. Secure a position on your opponent from which it is very difficult for him to defend himself.
3. Give it all you have so you can put the man out quickly.
4. Release pressure on your opponent *immediately* after he goes out. *No exceptions!!!*

Technique 1: *Kata Juji-jime (Single Cross Choke)*

Application

Under the general title of *juji-jime*, there are three varieties: (1) *kata juji-jime*, in which one arm holds the collar and the other places the edge of the hand against the side of the neck; (2) *gyaku juji-jime*, in which both hands hold the collar and the *gi* itself presses against the sides of the neck; and (3) *nami juji-jime*, in which both hands cross over the windpipe and the edge of the hands create pressure on the sides of the neck.

In *kata juji-jime*, one hand holds the collar, the other uses the edge of the hand against the opponent's side of the neck (*photo 5-32* illustrates close-up of hand position).

1. The right hand holds inside the opponent's collar *(see photo 5-33)*.
2. The left hand is placed on the side of the neck *(see photo 5-34)*.
3. Pressure is applied when the opponent is on his back and you are on top of him. Pull hard with the right hand, drawing the collar across the side of the opponent's neck. Push hard with the left hand into the side of the opponent's neck.

Note: On all chokes, pressure is applied only on the sides of the neck to cut off blood supply to the brain for only a few seconds—never against the windpipe!

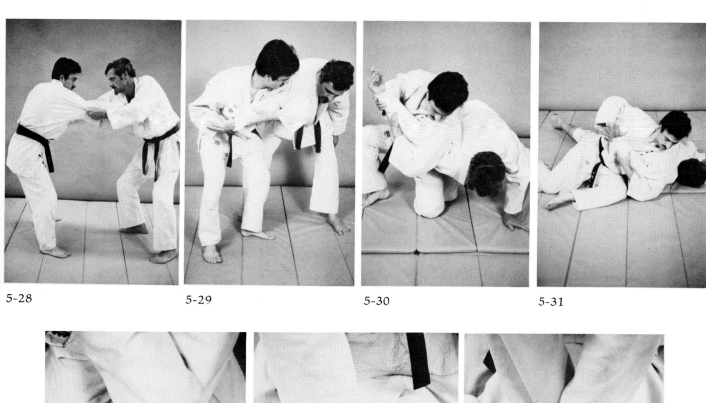

5-28   5-29   5-30   5-31

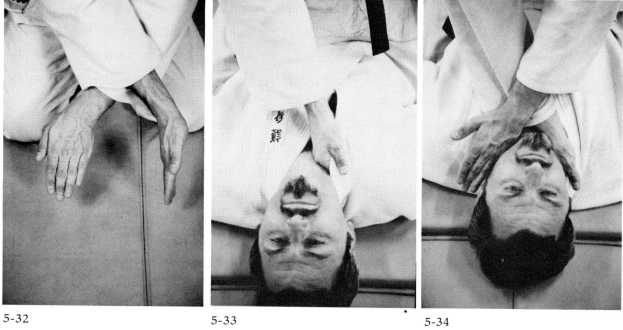

5-32   5-33   5-34

Technique 2: *Kuzure Kata Juji-jime* (Variation of Single Cross Choke)

Application

When you are on your back, and your opponent attempts a hold-down, apply a *kata juji-jime*, pulling your opponent in close to you. Pin his legs down with your legs to prevent him from wiggling out *(see photo 5-35)*.

Technique 3: *Gyaku Juji-jime* (Reverse Cross Strangle)

Application

This particular choke is extremely difficult to break out of once your opponent has secured a hold on you or once you have secured it on your opponent. Also, the *gyaku juji-jime* and the *kata juji-jime* can be substituted for one another. If one fails, you can always apply the other.

1. The hand position differs from *kata juji-jime* in that *both* hands grab the opponent's collar and choke him with his uniform *(see close-up of hand positions in photo 5-36)*.
2. The right hand grabs the inside of the opponent's collar *(see photo 5-37)*.
3. The left hand crosses the right hand and grabs the inside of the opponent's collar *(see photo 5-38)*.
4. Pressure is applied when the opponent is on his back (or you are on your back looking up to him). Pull hard with the hands, forcing the uniform to choke the sides of your opponent's neck.

Technique 4: *Hadaka Jime* (Naked Choke)

Application

This very powerful hold takes an opponent out in seconds.

1. Approach the opponent from the rear.
2. Wrap your arm around the opponent's neck, placing your elbow over his throat.
3. Grasp your wrist with your free hand.
4. Pressure is applied with a viselike action *(see photo 5-39)*.

Caution: Choking action is taken against the sides of the neck (using the forearm and upper arm). *Do not place the forearm against the throat as **DEATH** to the opponent can result.*

Technique 5: *Kuzure Hadaka Jime* (Variation of Naked Choke)

Application

This is the same as *hadaka* in concept. When your opponent is on all fours trying to get up, approach him from his head and wrap the arm around the neck, grabbing your wrist (or closed fist) for support *(see photo 5-40)*.

Technique 6: *Kataha-jime* (One-Wing Choke Hold)

Application

1. Approach your opponent from the rear.
2. Grasp his left lapel in your right hand.
3. Lift up his arm and wrap your left arm above his armpit (trapping his arm and hindering his motion). Place your left hand behind your opponent's neck.
4. Pressure is applied by pressing down and to the left side of your opponent's head and pulling the collar with your right hand across the opponent's neck *(see photo 5-41)*.

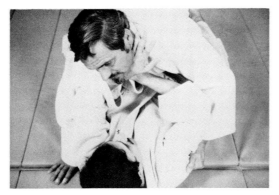

5-35

5-36

5-37

5-38

5-39

5-40

5-41

Technique 7: *Kuzure Kataha-jime 1* (First Variation of One-Wing Choke Hold)

Application

1. Start when your opponent goes to all fours to evade a pinning technique.
2. Grab the opponent's left lapel with your left hand *(see photo 5-42)*.
3. Place your right foot on the opponent's left knee, bringing him to the mat face first. Put your left knee on your opponent's right side to control his movement.
4. Place your right hand on the opponent's neck, trapping his right arm in a one-wing *(kataha)* position.
5. Pressure is applied by pulling on the left hand, drawing the opponent's collar across his neck, and pushing down with the right hand *(see photo 5-43)*.

Technique 8: *Kuzure Kataha-jime 2* (Second Variation of One-Wing Choke Hold)

Application

1. The opponent has gone on all fours to avoid a pinning technique.
2. Grasp his left lapel with your right hand at your opponent's right side *(see photo 5-44)*.
3. Roll over his back onto the mat, keeping a grip on your opponent's lapel. This will roll your opponent over and on top of you *(see photo 5-45)*.
4. Wrap your left arm around your opponent's left arm (into a one-wing position) and press the opponent's head down and to the right. At the same time, pull the opponent's lapel across his neck *(see photo 5-46)*.
5. Keep your left leg over the opponent to inhibit his escape.

Technique 9: *Okuri-eri-jime* (Lapel Strangle)

Application

This is an extremely effective choke that applies pressure to the sides of the neck and the throat in a safe manner.

1. Approach your opponent from behind.
2. Grab his right lapel with your left hand and his left lapel with your right hand *(see photo 5-47)*.
3. Apply pressure by drawing the lapels across the throat and side of the neck *(see photo 5-48)*.

5-42

5-43

5-44

5-45

5-46

5-47

5-48

Technique 10: *Kuzure Okuri-eri-jime* (Variation of Lapel Strangle)

Application

This is an excellent technique to apply when the opponent has gone on all fours and tucked himself tightly to evade a pinning technique.

1. Step in on your opponent's side.
2. *Stay close* and extend your legs as if riding a bike (like the *kesa gatame* position).
3. Bring your arms to the opponent's lapels and secure an *okuri-eri-jime* **(see photo 5-49)**.
4. Pressure is applied the same as for the *okuri-eri-jime*. The opponent is held stable by the foot position and body tightness.

Technique 11: *Sankaku-jime* (Triangular Strangle)

Application

This technique applies extreme pressure to the side of your opponent's neck and traps his arm as well. Unconsciousness occurs *very* quickly with this strangle.

1. You have been taken down to the ground, and your opponent is approaching you.

2. Move so that you place your feet in the direction of the approaching opponent.
3. Grab his right arm and draw him in, wrapping your legs around his neck and trapping his right arm.
4. When locking your feet, place your right instep just above your left back knee, locking your thighs in tight to the opponent and making sure his captured arm is tight into his neck.
5. Apply pressure by tensing the toes and pointing them straight up and bringing your thighs together *(see photo 5-50)*.

Technique 12: *Ushiro Sankaku-jime* (Rear Triangular Strangle)

Application

You have taken the opponent down, and you are holding on to his arm.

1. Get to the opponent's rear.
2. Pull the left arm toward you and lock his head by placing your right leg across his throat and securing a tight hold to the right leg with the left leg.
3. Keep your opponent's arm tight to his neck and apply pressure in the same manner as for the *sankaku-jime (see photo 5-51)*.

5-49

5-50

5-51

6 STRATEGY

Until 1961 the Japanese thought they were superior to any other nation in judo. But then, why not? They founded it, nourished it, and brought it to a level of international respect and fame.

The problem with this attitude, however, was that many high-ranking Japanese *judoka* did not take the efforts of non-Japanese *judoka* seriously (since they felt that *they* didn't take judo seriously).

This problem was solved when Anton Geesink of Holland defeated Koji Sone of Japan and became the "World Judo Champion." This defeat made the Japanese stand up and take notice of judo in the rest of the world.

What gave Geesink the ability to defeat the best and become the best? *Strategy!*—a plan of action that involved both physical and psychological factors. We will look at both.

SETTING A GOAL

There is a saying that goes something like this: winning is 25 percent skill and 75 percent determination.

Simply put, if you are determined to win, you can and will win. You can win as much and go as far as you desire to go. The key is to set a goal and stick with it: do everything physically and mentally possible to see that goal realized.

Sometimes this involves many sacrifices: special diets, vigorous workouts, holistic living. Attitude changes are also necessary. You must develop the mind of a winner and truly believe that you are capable of doing whatever your mind tells you to do.

This is easily said but sometimes very difficult to do. How do you start? First, set your goals and commit these goals to writing. Save that piece of paper.

If your goal is to become the champion of the world, then write it down on a piece of paper and put that piece of paper aside—but keep it in view.

Next, take out the pencil and write down what will be necessary, in your opinion, to become the world judo champion. Some suggestions on your list might be:

- Daily workouts of up to four hours each
- Special training seminars across the country
- Special weight training for strength
- Extra yoga training for mental/physical integration
- Supplementary reading on judo to see how others are doing it

Write each of these suggestions on its own piece of paper.

Next, for each of these ideas, write down how you intend to fulfill the goal. Example:

DAILY WORKOUTS OF UP TO FOUR HOURS EACH

PLAN OF ATTACK:
(1) Running 4 miles a day
(2) 1½ hours of *randori* training
(3) 1 hour of strength/conditioning exercises
(4) 30 minutes of yoga
(5) 45 minutes of *uchikomi* exercises
(6) More *randori*, etc.

SPECIAL SUBGOALS:
Start running 4 miles and build up to 10.

Do this with each of your goals, making them as detailed as possible. Next, make a special wall display for yourself for each of your original goals. This may be champion of the state, champion of the region, champion of the world; or they may be less competitive in nature—achieve my black belt, be the best in the school in both form and attitude, and/or execute the *nage-no-kata* (a judo *kata*) flawlessly.

Each goal will then be a poster of its own with the main goal lettered boldly at the top, with each part necessary to achieve the goal as subtitles, and finally, each activity necessary to achieve the subtitles in a list.

Display your set of posters so you can see them. Display them on the wall of your den, bedroom, etc. And, if it is OK with your *sensei*, display it in your *dojo*.

Displaying them is not enough, however. You must read them many times each day and begin to work on the steps necessary to make you successful at the facet of judo you are most involved in.

SLUMPS AND PLATEAUS

The hardest things for a *judoka* of advanced competitive skill to overcome are slumps and plateaus. Although each is defined differently, the psychological effect on the *judoka* is the same. The slump is a mental/physical rut that a *judoka* falls into because he does not have the self-discipline to go beyond it. The plateau is experienced when a *judoka* feels he has become as good as he can; although he doesn't stop training, he stops improving because he lacks the self-discipline to go beyond this stage.

The result is the same: no improvement! The secret to getting over slumps and plateaus is to study your goal charts and attack the goals again, this time with a different perspective. Do whatever it takes—play whatever mind games you have to play with yourself—but keep on training, even harder than before.

Of the two, the plateau is the hardest obstacle to overcome because it is tied into the human ego. We fall into this situation when we feel we are good but can't seem to defeat an opponent we consider better. So we say to ourselves, "This guy is just too good, so I'm giving up at second best." We soon convince ourselves that second best is OK and that number two is still damn good.

The point here is not to make winning all-important but to point out that the human animal is capable of accomplishing whatever he wishes if he desires so and sacrifices to do so. This determination, taught in the *dojo*, can be applied to any and all aspects of human life. Thus, the self-discipline of judo is a training tool for life.

Continuing with our example of the prospective world champion, he has two options: (1) stay where he is and never fulfill his true potential as a judoka or a human being; or (2) change his attitude and strive to be number one.

Changing your attitude in this sense can be very difficult. When training for the 1974 East Coast Judo Championships (an AAU event), I decided the only way to attain the skill I wanted was to increase my workouts (more on this later) and adopt a Zenlike mental attitude. This took the form of *mizu-no-kokoro* (mind like water) and what has been popularized by a motion picture called *Rocky III*, *"the eye of the tiger."*

The "eye of the tiger" represents the animal's ability to look at situations without preconceived thoughts about winning or losing. The tiger looks at his prey or his opponent indifferently. Whether it be rabbit or elephant, the tiger does his best with each foe, never sizing him up and never trying to guess his skill. He gives 100 percent effort each and every time. Again, *mizu-no-kokoro* is mind like water. It represents the still water's ability to see all objects around it undistorted. When the water is still (the mind is calm) all objects are seen as they truly are. However, when ripples enter the surface (preconceived thoughts entering the mind) the reflection is distorted; the mind is unable to see reality as it truly is.

The "mind like water" example can be compared directly to *mushin,* or the Zen concept of "no mind." Zen is an Eastern philosophy through which one seeks to see one's true potential. Zen is the immediate, unreflective grasp of reality, without logic and intellectualization—the realization of one's oneness with the universe. This is the preintellectual grasp of a child, but on a new level, that of the fullest development of man's logic, reason, and senses: his individuality.

Mushin, or Zen "no mind," says that a mind conscious of itself is a mind that is not disturbed by effects of any kind. If there is thought (e.g., "This opponent is too good. What shall I do?"), the "no mind" doesn't exist. A "no mind" keeps nothing in, like the tiger that sees all as it truly is (everything's true nature).

When "no mind" is attained, the *judoka* mind will flow freely from one object to another, flowing like a stream that fills every possible corner. For this reason the mind fulfills every function required of it.

However, when the flowing stops at any one point, the body freezes and the judoka fails. The wheel revolves only when the shaft is not too tightly attached to the axle. If the mind has something in it (preconceived thoughts of defeat), it will stop functioning and cannot hear, even when sound enters the ears; it cannot see, even when light flashes before the eyes. To have something in the mind means that it is preoccupied and has no time for anything else. *But to attempt to remove the thought already fills it with another something.*

Thus, the task is endless. It is best, therefore, not to enter a contest (or life in general) with preconceived thoughts. How do you achieve this? *Integration*—making the mind and body one with supplemental yoga training and meditation (see Chapter 3).

The best description of "no mind" was written by Yagyu Tajime no Kami, a seventeenth-century samurai.

> The uplifted sword has no will of its own. It is all of emptiness. It is like a flash of lightning. The man who is about to be struck down is also of emptiness, and so is the one who wields the sword. None of them are possessed of a mind of any substance. As each of them is of emptiness, the striking man is not a man, the sword is not a sword, and the "I" that is about to be cut down is like the splitting of spring breeze in a flash of lightning. When the mind does not "stop," the sword swinging can be nothing more than the blowing of the mind.

However, "no mind" is still not enough. The body must still be able to execute the techniques correctly and flawlessly.

Thus, a good strategist is aware of his own abilities and his weaknesses. He must appreciate the opponent's abilities and limitations; the knack for instinctively ("no mind") taking advantage of the opponent's vulnerabilities; the flexibility to change attack; and, most important, see with the eyes of the tiger, never fearing or sizing up an opponent—simply doing what has to be done to take him out.

TRAINING AND MORE TRAINING

The key to applying "no mind" is not only spiritual preparation but the physical ability to use the advanced strategic ability "no mind" gives you.

Training is essential and should take the following form:

- Yogic integration training
- Traditional conditioning, flexibility, and strength drills
- Weight training (in moderation for strength, not for "the body beautiful")
- *Uchikomi* exercises
- *Sutegeiko* exercises
- *Randori*
- Running or stationary bicycle training

The first two items are explained extensively in Chapter 3, and the third is beyond the scope of this text (I recommend one of the excellent weight-training books published by Contemporary Books, Inc.).

Uchikomi can be done one of two ways: static and dynamic. In static *uchikomi* the opponent stands still for you and you practice the *kuzushi* and *tsukuri* of throws, but not the *kake*. In other words, move in for the throw, start the throwing action, but *do not throw him.*

In dynamic *uchikomi* the opponent moves around so you are forced to use more off-balancing to secure the throwing position.

Uchikomi develops superior reflexes, builds the muscles, adds speed to your techniques, and promotes endurance.

Sutegeiko is perhaps the single most important training tool one can use for competition, excluding, of course, *randori* (by far the most important *physical* conditioning tool for competition). What makes *sutegeiko* so useful is that you can train in it with a "no mind" perspective. Also, the yogic integration that you have worked so hard to attain in static postures can now be practiced with movement.

Again, *sutegeiko* can be practiced in static or dynamic fashion. When done statically, you execute the entire throw *without resistance from your partner.* (However, he should not fall for you.)

In dynamic *sutegeiko* the partner moves about and you throw him—relying more on off-balancing than on static *sutegeiko*. As in *uchikomi*, the opponent offers no resistance to the thrower (*tori*), nor does he fall for him.

Uchikomi can be practiced in several ways: to build power, to build speed, and to build technique.

Building technique is the purpose of the standard *uchikomi* mentioned earlier. To build power, try performing *uchikomi* on a tree around which you have wrapped your *obi* (belt). The ends of the *obi* act like the opponent's arms; the tree itself is the opponent's body. This develops a great ability to uproot a man from the mat.

Speed *uchikomi* is performed by practicing how fast you can move in on your opponent. An expert can perform 60 *uchikomi* per minute (one throw per second).

Randori is practiced by two *judoka* attacking and defending each other at will. It is usually an all-out effort by each *judoka* but can be modified (as in controlled *randori*, where one person tries to evade an attack with all his effort, but once the *tsukuri* is in, the partner falls; in this type of *randori* one person is designated *tori* and the other *uke*).

Randori gives the *judoka* a feeling of body dynamics and gives him the practical experience of bodily contact for contests or self-defense situations. Although one does not strike or kick in *randori*, the feeling and sensitivity for body movement is essential for self-defense.

Randori requires only two things: a *judogi* and a *tatami* (mat), making it very simple to begin practice. Although most competitors use only three or four throwing techniques for winning, during *randori* it is important to become successful with *all* throwing methods.

Hayward Nishioka, former AAU national judo champion and author of more than 100 articles on judo and the best-selling book, *The Judo Textbook* (Ohara Publications, Inc.), gives some specific tips on randori practice:

1. See how many times you can throw your opponent during a practice session.
2. Give yourself one point for each time you throw your opponent and see how many points you can accumulate.
3. See how many times you can execute the same throw during a *randori* session.
4. Try throwing your opponent as soon as you grab his *gi*.
5. Try various combinations of techniques until they become second nature.
6. Practice *randori* until you can no longer stand.

The last physical training method to discuss is running and/or stationary bicycle training. Both give the *judoka* training in aerobic activity, preventing him from getting fatigued quickly during judo practice. Both of these exercises will increase the heart's ability to pump blood per heartbeat. In addition, more oxygen will be passed into the bloodstream, preventing lactic acid buildup in the muscle fibers. This will result in muscles that don't tire as quickly.

The last benefit of this type of aerobic training is that the heart will be required to beat less frequently per minute to supply oxygen to the body, making the *judoka* better able to stand the physical stress of competition.

Strategy is much more than a mental attitude; it is a complete plan of action involving mental, emotional, and physical factors.

Remember, the winning *judoka* is always a strategist.

7
AN AFTERWORD

Although we mentioned some of the philosophy of Dr. Kano in Chapters 1 and 2, it is very important to conclude our examination of fundamental judo technique by looking into the humanitarian philosophy of Jigoro Kano.

Dr. Kano established three principles for his judo to be used as a means of complete physical/mental education: *jitta kyoe, jiko no kansei,* and *seiryoku zenryo.*

Jitta kyoe is a maxim translating roughly as "mutual benefit and welfare." *Jitta kyoe* relates directly to *jiko no kansei,* which means "striving for perfection."

When one strives for perfection he must be of sound health, excellent character, patience, honesty, loyalty, and intelligence. One should attain, through perfection, wealth (not necessarily in terms of *money*) and solid being. Judo was a means of attaining complete perfection.

However "mutual benefit and welfare" tempered the "perfection" maxim by seeing that the individual did not concern himself solely with himself, but saw to the welfare and benefit of others. Thus the idea of give and take: judo for the good of all.

Last, *seiryoku zenryo* was defined earlier in this book to mean "maximum efficiency." It is the ability to use energy effectively with the least effort (see Chapters 1 and 2). But in addition to physical interpretations, Kano stressed the principle in everyday life, making one achieve the highest goals through the use of positive energy.

Kano's judo developed a threefold path:

BODY
CHARACTER
INTELLECT

Body: Kano said that the body is the instrument of life. Therefore, the body is the temple of existence. The necessity for physical fitness, then, is self-evident. The physical aspects of judo train the body to its fullest capacity.

Character: Kano said, "We live in the world of humans; we must therefore follow the rules of humans. If we lose our desire to live as humans, we lose our worth." Judo is a method of developing sound character. Proper training can teach us the principles of life.

Intellect: "Intelligence builds character," said Kano. Thus, it is all-important to develop our intellect as well as our bodies and characters in order to be complete human beings. Judo is also a means of building the intellect; it gives us the determination and the self-discipline to learn all that we can in all aspects of existence.

The combined realization of character, body, and intellect makes a judo player a judo champion.

APPENDIX I:
THE RANKING SYSTEM

According to Donn F. Draeger, a noted writer and pioneer of many of the more ancient of the *bugei* (martial arts) and *budo* (martial ways), in judo, "Rank follows the man."

Since judo is a product of Japanese culture and is a modernization of *jujutsu,* a product of Japanese feudalism, it is not surprising to find different ranks to denote progress. The matters of genealogy and court rank were very important in feudal Japan. Each class was given a certain status; within each group, varying status levels were also assigned.

The most important of these groups, as far as judo is concerned, is the samurai.

The samurai was immensely proud of his ancestral heritage, which, more often than not, was rooted in nobility. Expertise in martial arts became a privilege of only the samurai class. Why? Because the nobles were concerned with matters of state and power, and the classes below the samurai (merchants, craftsmen, etc.) were not allowed to carry swords. Thus, numerous martial ways and traditions (*ryu*) were established to perpetuate the martial arts. It became natural for

each of these traditions to have its own method of denoting technical progress.

However, technical skill was not the only requirement for each ranking. Other requirements were maturity, dedication, responsibility, and social conscience. The most important of the martial arts schools of the era established a ranking system based on four levels:

1. *Oku-iri* (entrance to secrets). This was the first credential. It is comparable today to a first-degree black belt. It signified that the bearer was an accomplished samurai and an instructor of the tradition he trained in.

2. *Moku-roku* (cataloged). This was a middle step that signified the samurai as being an *accomplished* samurai warrior (fighter) and an excellent teacher. This is equivalent to a second- or third-degree black belt.

3. *Menkyo* (licensed). A highly skilled technician and a seasoned warrior; equals today's fourth- through sixth-degree black belts.

4. *Kaiden* (everything passed). This was the master technician and superior warrior. This equals our seventh- to tenth-degree black belts.

Dr. Kano, however, did not apply the *jujutsu* ranking system to his art because he wanted to be completely separate from the *jujutsu* of his era (see Chapter 1 for explanation). Instead, Dr. Kano pioneered the *kyu-dan* ranking system that is followed today by all practicing *judoka* as well as those of *aikido* and karate. By awarding class (*kyu*), Kano identified his ungraded (*mudansha*) exponents; and by awarding grade (*dan*), he identified his graded (*yudansha*) students.

When Dr. Kano instituted the *kyu-dan* ranking system he had specific goals in mind. The most important of these was realizing that judo was much more than combat or sport. It was a way of developing the entire person: physical, mental, and spiritual. If a student did not develop in each of these three areas, he *did not* advance in the ranking system (see the "Three Culture Principles" in Chapter 2).

Judo training in Kano's era began with: (1) sensible physical training; (2) perfection of the self; (3) *randori* (free fighting); (4) *kata* (form exercise); and (5) *shiai*, or contest. The percentage of time to be devoted to each of these entities was 80 percent for *randori,* 17 percent for *kata,* and 3 percent for contests. Thus, competitive judo was not the intended goal or endpoint of judo training. It was, rather, only the means to the end of total self-perfection. Training in contest skill alone, without regard to true technique (*randori*) or form (*kata*), would not develop the three culture principles so important to Kano.

Judo rank is issued not only on the performance of technical ability, but by the realization of the three culture principles. The belt ranks themselves are in degrees of color intensity, proceeding from very light or empty (white) to dense (black).

It is because of this high ideal that many new organizations have sprung up around the world in an attempt to reestablish the high ideals that Kano wanted for his judo. These new organizations feel that the older bodies are too competitive by nature and should be in charge of sport only.

Regardless of the organization one is affiliated with, the ranking system is pretty much standardized (it is the *requirements* for each rank that aren't). Another point that is universally accepted (but rarely practiced) is that a man does not prepare or shoot for a rank; the rank is awarded when the man has achieved or "reached" the level necessary to warrant the rank. That is why Mr. Draeger says, "Rank follows the man"—*not* "Man runs after rank."

Judo rank is broken down into three categories: *yonen* (under 12 years old), *shomen* (13–17 years old), and *senior* (18 and up). Based on age, various ranks transfer and are referred to as rank conversions. Although the following is the form of rank colors accepted by the USJF (United States Judo Federation) and the USJA (United States Judo Association), the teacher still has the right to alter the pattern somewhat. For example, I have all my students, regardless of age, use the *color scheme* of the *yonen* ranking; however, I am still obligated to follow the conversions for my younger students.

BELT COLORS

Rank	Yonen	Shomen	Senior
Rokkyu	white	white	white
Gokyu	yellow	yellow	white
Yonkyu	orange	orange	green
Sankyu	green	green	brown
Nikyu	blue	blue	brown
Ikkyu	purple	purple	brown
Shodan	—	black	black #1
Nidan	—	—	black #2
Sandan	—	—	black #3
Yondan	—	—	black #4
Godan	—	—	black #5
Rokudan	—	—	red/white or black
Shichidan	—	—	red/white or black
Hachidan	—	—	red/white or black
Kudan	—	—	red or black
Judan	—	—	red

RANK CONVERSION*

Yonen	Shonen	Senior
Rokkyu		
Gokyu		
Yonkyu	Rokkyu	
Sankyu	Gokyu	
Nikyu	Yonkyu	Rokkyu
Ikkyu	Sankyu	Gokyu
	Nikyu	Yonkyu
	Ikkyu	Sankyu
		Nikyu
		Ikkyu

_____

* In essence, this means that if, for example, a child is 12 and holds a *yonkyu,* when he turns 13 years of age he will convert to *rokkyu.*

There are basic requirements for each rank, and to list each requirement from each organization would be far beyond the scope of this text. However, there are *generalizations* that are recognized throughout most judo organizations. These are: general requirements, promotion boards, time in grade (based on candidate classification), and tournament points.

General requirements are moral character, attitude, and maturity; competitive ability with technical proficiency; contributions to judo with time in grade; and reccommendation from the student's instructor.

The promotional board is a group of black-belt examiners a student must perform in front of to prove his technical ability. This is usually only enforced with promotion to black belt.

Time in grade is based on a candidate's classification; that is, competitor or noncompetitor. A competitor is required to spend less time in grade and will be given great status for his competitive accomplishments toward promotion. A noncompetitor is an active student who participates on all levels of the art except competition. A noncompetitor is graded the same as a competitor except that greater technical knowledge is required with greater time in rank. (See chart below.)

Tournament points refer to actual tournaments won by a *judoka* of competitor status. The greater the points earned, the less time required on each rank toward advancement.

MINIMUM TIME IN GRADE AND TOURNAMENT POINT CHART*

Promotion to rank of:	Non-competitor	5 points	10 points	15 points	20** points	Minimum Age
Gokyu	4 mo.	4 mo.	4 mo.	4 mo.	4 mo.	—
Yonkyu	6 mo.	6 mo.	6 mo.	6 mo.	6 mo.	—
Sankyu	9 mo.	6 mo.	6 mo.	3 mo.	3 mo.	—
Nikyu	1 yr.	9 mo.	6 mo.	3 mo.	3 mo.	—
Ikkyu	2 yrs.	1 yr.	9 mo.	6 mo.	3 mo.	—
Shodan	3 yrs.	2 yrs.	1 yr.	9 mo.	6 mo.	15 yrs. old
Nidan	4 yrs.	3 yrs.	2 yrs.	1½ yrs.	1 yr.	17 yrs. old
Sandan	6 yrs.	4 yrs.	3 yrs.	2½ yrs.	1½ yrs.	18 yrs. old
Yondan	8 yrs.	5½ yrs.	4 yrs.	3 yrs.	2 yrs.	21 yrs. old
Godan	10 yrs.	6½ yrs.	5 yrs.	4 yrs.	3 yrs.	22 yrs. old
Rokudan	12 yrs.	8 yrs.	6 yrs.	5 yrs.	4 yrs.	27 yrs. old
Shichidan	15 yrs.	10 yrs.	8 yrs.	6 yrs.	5 yrs.	

* Notes:
  1. Time in grade is *not* cumulative. It is time spent in present grade *only*.
  2. Tournament points can be counted only once and cannot be carried over to the next rank.
  3. These are requirements of the United States Judo Federation and are not the sole requirements throughout all judo.
** Called *batsugun,* a term for an extraordinary judo competitor.

APPENDIX II:

NUTRITIONAL INFORMATION FOR JUDO TRAINING

The process by which one receives and utilizes food is called *nutrition*; and the life-sustaining constituents in food are called *nutrients*.

During one's average lifetime of 70 years, a 165-pound person will eat 35 tons of food. Clearly there is a great need to become knowledgeable about food, which is ingested in such large quantities.

A *judoka* who truly wishes to be above average in technique and attitude would do well to learn about nutrition.

The body needs some 50 or so nutrients in order to function properly. These include amino acids (protein), carbohydrates, fats, minerals, vitamins, and water. We will look at each of these as they relate to judo training.

AMINO ACIDS (PROTEIN)

Every living creature requires protein for existence since so much of the body is made up of it (a typical 150-pound person is composed of about 94 pounds of water, 27 pounds of protein, 23 pounds of fat, 5 pounds of mineral [mostly in bone], one pound of carbo-

hydrates, and less than one ounce of vitamins). Skin, hair, nails, muscles, cartilage, tendons, blood, and the organic structure of bones are largely made up of protein.

Chemically, protein is made up of smaller units called *amino acids*. There are 22 different amino acids that are required by the body to function. Eight of these must come from food and are thus called *essential amino acids* (isoleucine, leucine, lysine, methionine, phenylalanine, threonine, tryptophan, and valine); the rest can be synthesized by the body itself and are termed *nonessential*.

Proteins from meat, fish, poultry, eggs, and milk supply all the essential amino acids. Protein from cereal grains, vegetables, and fruits also supply valuable amounts of amino acids, but they must be eaten in complements; that is, you must select two or three forms of nonmeat protein that *together* supply all eight essential amino acids.

The *judoka* needs extra amounts of protein at the early stages of training to repair body tissues that are damaged during *ukemi-waza* (breakfalls) and *randori* (free throwing). This author believes in a fish-and-vegetable ap-

147

proach to protein supplementation because of the high-quality amino acids and the low fat content.

CARBOHYDRATES

Carbohydrates come in three basic forms: starches, sugars, and celluloses. Celluloses, along with hemicelluloses, lignin, pectin, and curtin, furnish fibrous bulk in the diet. These complex substances are found in the cell walls of various plants, and the quantity of each substance depends on the specific plant and may vary with each species.

The most common type of carbohydrate is found in starches and sugars; these are the major source of energy for the active *judoka*. It takes about two pounds of carbohydrates to provide a 160-pound competitor with fuel for a two-hour workout. In the absence of carbohydrate supply, the body will break down fat and protein and convert it to sugar for energy supply. Some consider this a very dangerous situation, which makes the low-carbohydrate, high-protein diets followed by some *judoka* potentially dangerous.

When a diet is low in carbohydrates and high in protein (and, in some diets, high or middle in fat), the body is forced to depend on fat reserves since the carbohydrates are burnt rapidly, as is glucose in the blood. The fatty acids derived from the fat reserve burn inefficiently and produce acid metabolites called *ketones*. This results in a condition called *ketosis*. Although *ketosis* will effect weight loss and reduce hunger, it also changes the pH of blood. If the blood becomes acidic enough, one can go into *ketosis* shock (a very real possibility since judo is an extremely strenuous sport), which can be fatal.

Except for milk and milk products, which contain sugar and lactose, nearly all carbohydrate sources a *judoka* should ingest are from plants: grains, fruits, vegetables. Use of refined sugar (see "Sugar" section) is not recommended for a serious holistic competitor. A good natural substitute is honey.

FATS

Fats are complex food components composed of glycerol and essential fatty acids. Fats can be saturated or unsaturated, which refers to the structure of the hydrogen atom. Saturated fats increase the cholesterol content of the blood and lead to heart disease (sources being beef, pork, and most animal meats, including dairy products). Unsaturated fats, found in fish and vegetables, do not add to cholesterol levels and are believed by some to reduce those levels. The *judoka* should not eliminate all fat from his diet but should instead choose meals that keep the levels moderate and contain some amount of unsaturated fat.

Fat supply is essential for a *judoka* who plans a career in competition. Fats are in essence concentrated forms of body energy (270 calories per ounce) that have reached an inactive (stored) state. The body will rely on these stored energy sources when it needs more energy. Having a moderate supply of stored energy will give a *judoka* the edge in a throw-or-be-thrown situation, when energy levels are nearly depleted.

Unsaturated fats (polyunsaturated) are a good source of fat, but the food industry has never been exactly crazy about them. They talk and talk about how wonderful these fats are, then remove as many as possible in order to increase the shelf life of products. What they don't remove they combine with commercial antioxidants in such a way as to protect them from both rancidity in the bottle and absorption in our stomachs. And then there is hydrogenation. Hydrogenated oils are simply unsaturated fats that have been saturated, filling them with hydrogens. This is done to give them a thick spreadability (as in peanut butter and margarine). One point here for the *judoka*: by adding hydrogen you are in essence adding more energy value to the food; however, if you are getting enough energy from the food you eat, it is best to stay away from hydrogenated foods.

MINERALS

The body requires minerals for several reasons: skeletal development, enzyme efficiency, and general metabolic stability, giving strength to body tissues. The ultimate source of minerals is soil; thus, plants are our best source in most cases. There are 21 mineral elements essential in nutrition: calcium, phosphorus, sulfur, potassium, chlorine, sodium, magnesium, iron, fluorine, zinc, copper, iodine, chromium, cobalt, silicon, vanadium, tin, selenium, manganese, nickel, and molybdenum (in order of decreasing importance to the adult human).

Calcium

One of the most important mineral supplements for a *judoka* is calcium. Calcium phosphate is the main structural ingredient of our bones: 40 percent calcium, 45 percent phosphate, 13 percent hydroxyl groups, 1 percent magnesium, and smaller amounts of sodium, strontium, citrate, and carbonate (to make up calcium phosphate).

The importance of calcium is driven home by the fact that, unique among minerals, calcium is regulated by hormones. There are many hormones involved in this, including hydroxylated vitamin D, parathyroid hormone, and thyrocalcitonin.

An active *judoka* will use up a large portion of calcium in his workouts, and it is very wise to take calcium supplements during periods of heavy sweating. (An active *judoka* may need as much as 1,200 mg of calcium per day.)

Phosphorus

Second to calcium in abundance in bones and teeth, phosphorus receives very little attention by nutritionists because it is a universal cell component available in all foods. Phosphorus is an essential component of nucleic acids and phospholipids of cell membranes.

Sulfur

Occurring principally as a constituent of cystine (an amino acid), sulfur is present in all proteins and is essential in skin and hair.

Magnesium

About 60 percent of body magnesium is found in bones and teeth. Among the other places, 26 percent is found in the muscles and the rest in body fluids and soft tissues. Magnesium works with calcium in getting the muscles to work. Calcium allows muscles to contract when the brain so orders, and magnesium allows them to stretch out again when the job is done. If there is insufficient magnesium, the muscles will twitch and tremor, and—if severe enough—spasms will occur. It is therefore essential to get a large amount of calcium and magnesium in our diets. The more we use our muscles and the more we sweat (as in a very heavy workout), the more we need these nutrients. Magnesium is found in nuts, whole grains, and dark green vegetables. About 450 mg of magnesium is needed per day when workouts are intensive (350 mg during nonworkout days).

Potassium, Sodium, and Chlorine

These three minerals are used in many bodily activities, but for the *judoka* we are concerned with the fact that they maintain normal muscle stability.

With all that has been written about salt (sodium chloride) in recent years (and most of it bad), we need sodium in large quantities if we sweat greatly during workouts and if we work out more than three times per week. In fact, water intoxication will occur if a large quantity of water is taken without some salt in the diet after a severe workout during which one sweats enormously (as one does in hot weather).

Potassium completes the muscle minerals. It acts like magnesium but is much more active in promoting relaxation. Potassium deficiency will cause tremors in the muscles, with lack of coordination, extreme fatigue, and lack of muscle strength. Potassium is lost in sweat and should be replenished after hard workouts. Kelp, soybeans, bananas, and pistachio nuts are good rich sources of potassium, as is sea salt.

Iron

Most of the body's iron exists in the blood where, in the form of hemoglobin or erythrocytes, it nourishes the body cells with oxygen. A wise *judoka* will be certain to get enough iron in his diet.

Manganese

Although it is sometimes used in place of magnesium by the body, manganese is generally involved in carbohydrate metabolism. Deficiency can impair the senses of vision, hearing, and smell. Generally at least 5 mg of manganese is required per day.

VITAMINS

Vitamins are present in most foods we eat and are essential for normal metabolic function as well as the maintenance of tissue structure and function. With few exceptions, the body cannot synthesize vitamins; they must be supplied in diet and/or supplements. Certain vitamins such as K, thiamine, folacin, and B_{12} may be formed by bacteria in the intestinal tract (yogurt intake helps this process greatly, and it is recommended that the *judoka* eat pure yogurt at least four times a week). It is also known that vitamin A, choline, and niacin can be formed if their precursors are supplied. Vitamin D can be synthesized by the skin upon exposure to sunlight (however, this is a very uncertain way to get this vitamin; it should be supplemented). Since I have mentioned supplements, it should be noted that there is no evidence *yet* that natural vitamins are better than synthetic ones; however, this author prefers natural, perhaps only because I am very tired of the whole "artificial" syndrome.

Vitamin A

Vitamin A has been called *retinol* because it is needed for vision (retina). There are two types of vision, and for each there is a different type of cell in the retina to do the job. Cone cells respond to colors and require a lot of light to do so. Rod-shaped cells, on the other hand, are not color-sensitive and are able to function even in dark areas. The rod-shaped cells depend especially on vitamin A. This vitamin is also important for growth in the skeletal and soft tissues. Fish oils are the best source of this vitamin.

The B Complex

The B vitamins in general play a very important role in the metabolic process of all living cells by serving as cofactors in various enzyme systems involved with the oxidation of food and production of energy. The B vitamins are discussed below.

B_1 (Thiamine)

Thiamine is very much dependent on the intake of magnesium and manganese; without them, B_1 can't function. Thiamine is used for many things in the body, but for the *judoka* the following two are important: (1) Thiamine is essential for nerve fibers so they can properly transmit their commands. Thiamine tightly holds negatively charged phosphates against the inside of nerve membranes; there they maintain electric tension so messages can go from one nerve strain to the next. (2) Thiamine deficiency causes cramps in the muscle tendons, making muscles work less efficiently.

B_2 (Riboflavin)

Riboflavin is essential to proper enzyme function and (of interest to the *judoka*) energy transfer. Riboflavin is rich in most foods we eat, and deficiency rarely occurs.

B₃ (Niacin)

Without niacin, the 200 or so enzymes in the body would begin to close shop. This means that dehydrogenation reactions, whether for energy gathering, or making compounds essential to the body's operation, come to a virtual standstill.

There are two other aspects of niacin that relate more specifically to the *judoka*'s needs. First, research at the University of Rochester has found that niacin helps the body heal bruises, so extra amounts of B_3 can be taken to get over the soreness of a recent bout or heavy training session. Second, niacin is believed to act as a natural tranquilizer, helping the body keep calm in stress situations.

A word of warning: megadoses of niacin raise histamine levels in the body. Histamine forces water to leak out of the blood plasma into tissues, causing them to swell and mucus to build up. Therefore, individuals who suffer from allergies and hay fever should take only the Recommended Daily Requirement.

B₅ (Pantothenic Acid)

This is one B vitamin the *judoka* should know about because this one is responsible for energy and a deficiency leads to immediate decay.

The reason for this is that virtually all of the energy your body gets, be it from proteins, fats, or carbohydrates, gets locked up somewhere along the line in the body as acetate. So the process of extracting energy from these nutrients involves extracting them from an acetate state. B_5 is responsible for this. Without it, the body wears down, grows fatigued, and may even die.

Good sources are in supplements, royal bee jelly, rice, brewer's yeast, and soybeans.

B₆ (Pyridoxine)

Although this B vitamin has numerous uses in the body, a specific benefit for the *judoka* is its ability to develop a healthy heart and a strong circulatory system. This is accomplished with another nutrient, trypto-phan, which mixes with B_6 and helps prevent the blood vessels from developing blockages. Clear vessels promote better blood flow, which promotes better all-around athletic performance.

B₁₂ (Cobalamin)

B_{12} is so complex a vitamin that no plant or animal on the face of the earth can make it for itself. Where does it come from? Bacteria, plain and simple, and bacteria in the intestines should be able to supply the body with enough B_{12}, right? Not exactly! Bacteria love B_{12} themselves and usually eat more than they give to the body. Deficiency of B_{12} can lead to pernicious anemia (fatal), fatigue, and nervousness. Best sources for non-meat-eaters is yogurt, tempeh; for meat eaters, seafood.

Biotin

Biotin is a coenzyme that helps the body use its fuel more efficiently. Athletes use biotin in megadoses to increase energy and stamina. They report great success with it.

B₁₅ (Pangamic Acid)

Pangamic acid is believed to increase the body's efficiency of oxygen transportation. This results in greater endurance during sport competitions. Again, athletes report great success with megadoses of this nutrient. In the Soviet Union B_{15} is a regular part of an athlete's diet.

Vitamin C (Ascorbic Acid)

Although small amounts of vitamin C are stored in the liver, this nutrient must be replenished daily. Vitamin C is generally believed: (1) to help prevent the common cold (in megadoses); (2) to be associated with slowing down the aging process as an antioxidant; and (3) to help form and maintain cementing material that holds body cells together and strengthens the walls of blood vessels.

Vitamin D (Calciferol)

Vitamin D is essential in building strong bones to withstand the rigors of judo training (especially the falling). Food sources include milk with added D, and supplements. Natural sources include direct sunlight (ultraviolet) on the skin, but, as mentioned earlier, since many factors screen out the ultraviolet rays (atmosphere, glass, etc.), it is an unreliable source.

Vitamin E (Tocopherol)

Vitamin E is essential in producing energy for the *judoka's* active muscles. It has also been related to delaying the aging process. I always suggest that the competitive *judoka* supplement his diet with vitamin E. Noncompetitive *judoka* need not do so.

WATER

All too often, judo players neglect the intake of extra amounts of water to supplement their training. To be a complete *judoka* involves more than just training a few times a week and entering a few contests now and then. A complete *judoka* considers judo his "way of life," and each and every moment of his life is guided by his principles of judo. His diet, his attitude, even his performance on the job is a direct result of his mental and physical training.

Therefore, proper diet and supplementation (usually in the form of pills/tablets) is essential for a holistic approach. However, you must be sure to get *extra* amounts of water each day. When you are working out, you need six to eight glasses of water (maybe more, if one is an excessive sweater, like I am) per day. When you are taking a break from the *dojo* for a day, at least four glasses are required. This helps the body clear away waste and restores the individual to proper functioning.

OTHER NUTRITIONAL CONSIDERATIONS

Although the following are not all considered essential nutrients, they are important topics of interest for the well-rounded, nutritionally conscious *judoka*.

Cholesterol

Cholesterol is not a fat, though it is usually considered one. In reality, it is more like a sticky syrup or wax that doesn't dissolve very easily in the bloodstream. It is found in animal cells and is an essential component of brain and nerve cells. Cholesterol helps make bile acids for digestion and steroid hormones (e.g., progesterone). Cholesterol in the skin surface cells helps make them more resistant to certain chemical infections.

Although it is an essential body nutrient, cholesterol has become a controversial topic because of its role in blocking the blood vessels, increasing blood pressure, and ultimately leading to heart attack.

Rigorous judo activity helps the body build levels of HDL, or high lipoproteins, which transport cholesterol out of the blood vessels where it does its harm.

Thus, judo, because it rates in the top three as a beneficial exercise for the cardiovascular system, is an excellent activity in aiding the body's fight against heart disease. Reduced fat intake also helps a lot.

Sugar

Sugar is a carbohydrate and a major source of energy for human beings. There are many types of sugar: table sugar (sucrose), milk sugar (lactose), and malt sugar (maltose). These sugars are considered disaccharides because they are atomically made of two sugar molecules. The monosaccharides are glucose (blood sugar), fructose (fruit sugar), and galactose (produced in the body from milk sugar).

Any concentrated sugars, including sucrose, honey, and syrups (molasses, brown sugar syrup, maple syrup), have a deleterious effect in excessive quantities. The only time their effect is harmless is when certain sugars are ingested in conjunction with heavy workouts, when the body can use the sugar energy immediately. It is advisable, if you are taking this approach, to use natural sugars that immediately enter the bloodstream in the form of glucose (blood sugar). These are fructose (usually taken in tablet form, since eating fruits—the source of this sugar—adds bulk to the stomach), honey, or maple syrup.

It is not advisable to eat candy bars and the like before a workout because the sugars in the candy will not enter into the bloodstream immediately, and when they do their effect lasts only a very short time and you actually feel more fatigued after "coming down" from the sugar than before you took it in the first place. Stick to honey!

Caffeine

Over the course of my competitive career, I have seen many *judoka* taking caffeine pills before a match. Their reasoning was that it was a "natural" high rather than using drugs like "speed" for the same results. However, one need not take anything if one's diet is correct and one's training is holistic.

However, caffeine does stimulate the central nervous system, which will overcome fatigue and tiredness. It will also pump more oxygen into the lungs, increase the metabolic rate, and increase urine production.

But with these seemingly beneficial aspects come increased pulse rate, irregular heartbeat (from excessive amounts over a long period of time), ulcers, insomnia, and severe anxiety. Get your high the natural way by getting all your proper nutrients. Stay away from this one.

Bee Pollen

This one could take a book of its own to explain, so I'll keep it short. Each of my orange-belt students on up are required to start taking bee pollen and royal jelly. The reasons are many but can be narrowed down to one sentence: increased performance. They have achieved better stamina, better energy, and greater resistance to infections. I heartily recommend it, and it is available in most health food stores.

Oil of Evening Primrose

I recommend this one to students who are constantly getting sick after heavy workouts. This compound fights against fatigue and infection in the body. We have had great results from it and can recommend it highly.

A FINAL WORD

Nutrition is a way of coming back to a more natural body condition. It is a way of dealing with the specialized demands judo places on you. I carry this even further with my students and suggest that they look into alternate methods of healing whenever possible to treat minor and near-major athletic injuries. Certain conditions will always call for surgery, but many injuries can be corrected with a natural herbal approach. This topic is beyond the scope of this text, but I sincerely suggest that *judoka* look into it.

APPENDIX III:

INTERNATIONAL JUDO FEDERATION'S RULES OF SPORT JUDO

ARTICLE ONE: COMPETITION AREA

The competition area shall be a minimum of 14 m × 14 m and a maximum of 16 m × 16 m and shall be covered by *tatami* or a similar accepted substance.

The competition area shall be divided into two zones. The demarcation between these two zones shall be called the danger area and shall be indicated by a colored area, generally red, approximately one meter wide, forming part of or attached to the mat, parallel to the four sides of the competition area.

The area within and including the colored area shall be called the contest area and shall always be a minimum of 9 m × 9 m or a maximum of 10 m × 10 m. The area outside the colored area shall be called the safety area, and shall never be less than 2 meters, 50 cm wide.

The above competition area must be mounted on a resilient platform.

*These rules were adopted by the International Judo Federation at the Montreal Congress in 1976. Reprinted here by permission of the American Society of Classical Judoka.

ARTICLE TWO: UNIFORM

The contestants shall wear a *judogi* (costume) and, generally, as directed, shall also wear red or white tape or ribbon tied over the regulation belt.

The *judogi* must conform to the following regulations:

1. The jacket must be long enough to cover the hips and be tied at the waist by a belt.

2. The sleeves shall be loose and long enough to cover more than half of the forearm (there should be an opening of between three and five centimeters between the cuff and the largest part of the forearm).

3. The pants shall be loose and long enough to cover more than half of the lower leg (there should be an opening of eight centimeters between the bottom of the pants and the largest part of the calf).

4. The belt shall be tied with a square knot tight enough to prevent the jacket from being too loose and long enough to go twice round the body and leave about 20-30 centimeters protruding from each side of the knot when tied.

ARTICLE THREE: PERSONAL REQUIREMENTS

The contestant shall keep his nails cut short and shall not wear any metallic articles because they may cause injury to his opponent.

Any contestant whose hair, in the opinion of the referee/judges, is so long as to risk causing inconvenience to the other contestant, shall be required to securely tie back the hair.

ARTICLE FOUR: LOCATION

The contest shall be fought in the contest area. However, any technique applied when one or both of the contestants is outside the contest area shall not be recognized. That is to say that if one contestant shall have even one of his feet outside the contest area while standing, or more than half of his body outside the contest area whilst doing *sutemi-waza* (sacrifice throws) or *katame-waza* (ground-work), he shall be considered being outside the contest area.

However, where one contestant throws his opponent outside the contest area but himself stays in the area long enough for the effectiveness of the technique to be clearly apparent, the technique shall be recognized.

When *osaekomi-waza* (pinning) has been called, it may continue—until the time allowed for the *osaekomi* expires or *toketa* is called—so long as at least one player has any part of his body touching the contest area (including the danger zone).

ARTICLE FIVE: POSITION AT START OF THE CONTEST

The contestants shall stand facing each other at the center of the contest area and approximately 4 m apart and shall make a standing box.

The contest shall begin immediately after announcement of *hajime* (begin) by the referee and shall always begin with both contestants in the standing position.

ARTICLE SIX: START AND END OF CONTEST

The referee shall announce *hajime* (begin) in order to start the contest after the contestants have bowed to each other.

The referee shall announce *sore-made* (that is all) to end the contest.

At the end of the contest, all players shall return to start position, face each other and bow after the referee has announced the result of the contest.

ARTICLE SEVEN: RESULT

The result of the contest shall be judged on the basis of *nage-waza* (throwing techniques) and *katame-waza* (grappling techniques).

ARTICLE EIGHT: TERMINATION BY IPPON

The contest shall immediately end if and when one contestant scores *ippon* (full point).

ARTICLE NINE: ENTRY INTO *NE-WAZA* (GROUNDWORK)

The contestants shall be able to change from the standing position to *ne-waza* in the following cases, but should the employment of the technique not be continuous, the referee shall, at his option, order both contestants to resume the standing position.

1. When a contestant after obtaining some result of a throwing technique changes without interruption into *ne-waza* and takes the offensive.

2. When one of the contestants falls to the ground, following the unsuccessful application of a throwing technique, the other may follow him to the ground; or when one of the players is unbalanced and is liable to fall to the ground after the unsuccessful application of a throwing technique, the other may take advantage of his opponent's unbalanced position to take him to the ground.

3. When one contestant obtains some considerable effect by applying a *shime-waza* (chok-

ing) or *kansetsu-waza* (joint lock) in the standing position and then changes without interruption to *ne-waza*.

4. When one player takes his opponent down into *ne-waza* by the particularly skillful application of movement which, although resembling a throwing technique, does not fully qualify as such.

5. In any other case, where one player may fall down or be about to fall down not covered by the preceding subsections of this article, the other contestant may take advantage of his opponent's position to go into *ne-waza*.

ARTICLE TEN: DURATION

The duration of the contest shall be arranged in advance and shall be not less than three minutes and not more than twenty minutes. This arranged time may, however, be extended in certain special cases.

The time elapsed between the call "*matte*" and "*hajime*" and between "*sore-made*" and "*yo-shi*" by the referee shall not count as part of the duration of the contest.

ARTICLE ELEVEN: TIME SIGNAL

The end of the time allotted for the contest shall be indicated to the referee by the ringing of a bell or other similar audible method.

ARTICLE TWELVE: TECHNIQUE COINCIDING WITH THE TIME SIGNAL

Any throwing technique which is applied simultaneously with the bell (or other method of indicating end of time allotted) shall be recognized, and when an *osaekomi* (hold-down) is similarly announced simultaneously with the signal of the bell, etc., the time allotted for the contest shall be extended until either *ippon* is scored or the referee announces *toketa* (hold broken).

Further, any technique applied after the ringing of the bell or other device to signal end of contest shall not be valid, even if the referee has not at that time called *sore-made*.

ARTICLE THIRTEEN: *SONO-MAMA*

In any case where the referee wishes to stop the contest (e.g., in order to adjust the *judogi*, or address either of them without causing a change in their positions), he will call *sono-mama* (freeze). To start again, the referee will call *yoshi*.

NOTE: When this is called, be sure not to change any relative position; simply *freeze*.

ARTICLE FOURTEEN: RESPONSIBILITY

All actions and decisions taken in accordance with the majority of the three rules as in Article Twenty-Six by the referee and the judges shall be final and without appeal.

ARTICLE FIFTEEN: OFFICIALS

In general, a contest shall be conducted by one referee and two judges. However, in certain circumstances it may be permissible to have one referee and one judge or even just one referee.

ARTICLE SIXTEEN: POSITION AND FUNCTION OF REFEREE

The referee shall stay generally within the contest area and has the sole responsibility for conducting the contest and administering the judgment.

ARTICLE SEVENTEEN: POSITION AND FUNCTION OF THE JUDGES

The judges shall assist the referee and shall be positioned opposite each other at two corners outside the contest area.

Should a contestant be permitted to leave the competition area after the start of the contest (such as to change a dirty *judogi*), one judge must go and remain with him until he returns to the competition area.

ARTICLE EIGHTEEN: *IPPON* (FULL POINT)

The referee shall call *ippon* when, in his opinion, a throw or grappling technique applied by a contestant merits the score of *ippon*, and after stopping the contest shall return both players to the places in which they began the match.

In the case where both contestants score a result which would merit *ippon* simultaneously (for example, *shime-waza*), the referee shall announce *hiki-wake* (draw), and the players shall have the right to fight the contest again where necessary.

ARTICLE NINETEEN: *WAZA-ARI* (ALMOST *IPPON*)

The referee shall announce *waza-ari* when in his opinion the technique applied by the contestant merits the score of *waza-ari*.

Should one contestant gain a second *waza-ari*, the referee shall announce instead *waza-ari awasete* (two *waza-ari* score *ippon*), and after stopping the contest, shall return both players to start position.

ARTICLE TWENTY: *YUKO* (ALMOST *WAZA-ARI*)

The referee shall announce *yuko*, when in his opinion the technique merits such.

Should either contestant score two or further *yuko*, then the referee shall announce them as they are scored but shall not stop the contest for that reason.

Regardless of how many *yuko* are announced, no amount will be considered as being equal to *waza-ari*. The total number will be recorded, however, in the event a match is not won by *ippon* and a decision must be rendered.

ARTICLE TWENTY-ONE: *KOKA* (ALMOST *YUKO*)

The referee shall announce *koka* when in his opinion the technique merits such.

Should either contestant score two or more *koka*, then the referee shall announce them as they are scored but shall not stop the contest for that reason.

Regardless of how many *koka* are called, no amount will be considered as being equal to *yuko* or *waza-ari*. The total number of *kota* will be recorded and used in arriving at a decision whenever a contest is not won by *ippon*.

ARTICLE TWENTY-TWO: *SOGO-GACHI* (COMPOUND WIN)

The referee shall stop the contest and following the usual procedure indicate the winner after announcing *sogo-gachi* in the following cases:

1. Where one contestant has gained a *waza-ari* and his opponent subsequently receives a penalty of *keikoku* (warning).

2. Where one contestant whose opponent has already received a penalty of *keikoku* is subsequently himself awarded a *waza-ari*.

ARTICLE TWENTY-THREE: *OSAEKOMI* (HOLDING)

The referee shall announce *osaekomi* (holding) when in his opinion one contestant is successfully holding the other by a holding technique. The referee shall immediately announce *toketa* (hold broken) at any time after the announcement of *osaekomi* when he considers the hold broken.

ARTICLE TWENTY-FOUR: JUDGES' UNSOLICITED OPINIONS

Any judge shall have the right to voice a different opinion than a referee after holding up the appropriate signal. When both judges indicate the same opinion, the judge closest to the referee shall immediately approach him, requesting that he stop the contest and rectify the decision. If the second judge does not hold the same opinion as the first judge, he shall make no signal and the decision of the referee shall prevail.

ARTICLE TWENTY-FIVE: *HANTEI* (REQUEST FOR DECISION)

The referee shall announce *sore-made*, stop the contest, and return both contestants to start position.

Should the recorded scores indicate an advantage for either contestant on the following scale—one *waza-ari* wins over any number of *yukos* or *kokas*, and when no *waza-ari* has been scored, one or more *yukos* win over any number of *kokas*—the referee, having confirmed which contestant has won, will so indicate by raising his hand toward the winner.

Should the recorded scores either indicate no scores or be exactly the same under each heading (*waza-ari, yuko, kokas*), then the referee shall call *hantei* while raising his hand high in the air. The judges shall respond by raising a white or red flag above their heads in order to indicate which contestant they consider merits the decision. To indicate *hiki-wake* (draw) the judges will raise both colored flags at the same time.

ARTICLE TWENTY-SIX: DECLARATION OF DECISION

The referee shall add his own opinion to that indicated by the two judges and shall declare *hiki-wake* (draw) or *yusei-gachi* (superiority), according to the majority decision of all three.

Should the opinion of the two judges differ, the referee shall make the decision.

When there is only one judge, the referee shall take into consideration the opinion of the judge before announcing either *yusei-gachi* (superiority) or *hiki-wake* (draw).

ARTICLE TWENTY-SEVEN: APPLICATION OF *MATTE* (WAIT)

The referee shall announce *matte* (wait) in order to stop the contest temporarily in the following cases and to recommence the contest shall call *hajime*.

1. When one or both contestants go outside the contest area.

2. When one or both of the contestants perform or are about to perform one of the prohibited acts.

3. When one or both of the contestants are injured or take ill.

4. When it is necessary for one or both of the contestants to adjust their *judogi*.

5. When during *ne-waza* there is no apparent progress and the contestants lie still in a position such as *ashi-garami* (leg entanglement).

6. When one contestant remains in, or from *ne-waza* regains, a standing position and lifts his opponent, who is on his back with his leg(s) around any part of the standing contestant clear of the mat.

7. When in any other case the referee feels it is necessary in his opinion.

When the referee has called *matte*, the contestant(s) must either stand if being spoken to or having their clothing adjusted, or may sit cross-legged if a lengthy delay is envisaged.* Only when receiving medical attention should a contestant be permitted to take any other position.

ARTICLE TWENTY-EIGHT: DECISION AFTER PROHIBITED ACTS

Whenever a contest has been decided by *hansoku* (prohibitory act), *fusen* (default), *kiken* (withdrawal), injury, or accident, the referee shall indicate to the players the winner of the contest, or if the decision is *hiki-wake* (draw), the referee shall so announce the result.

ARTICLE TWENTY-NINE: OFFICIAL SIGNALS

- *Ippon:* Raise one hand, high above the head.

---

*NOTE: The American Society of Classical Judoka demands a contestant drop to his right knee.

- *Waza-Ari:* Raise one hand, palm down, sideways from the body at shoulder height.
- *Yuko:* Raise one hand, palm downward, sideways, 45 degrees from the body.
- *Koka:* Raise one arm bent with thumb toward the shoulder and elbow at hip level.
- *Osaekomi:* Point the arm out away from the body down toward the contestants, while facing the contestants and bending the body toward them.
- *Osaekomi Toketa:* Raise one hand to the front and wave it from right to left quickly two or three times.
- *Hiki-Wake:* Raise one hand high in the air and bring it down to the front of the body (with thumb edge up) and hold it there for a while.
- *Matte:* Raise one hand to shoulder height and with the arm approximately parallel to the mat, display the flattened palm of the hand with the fingers up to the timekeeper.
- To indicate a technique not considered valid, raise one hand above the head to the front and wave it from right to left two or three times.
- To indicate that, in your opinion, either or both of the contestants are guilty of noncombativity, raise both hands to chest height in front of your body and rotate both hands around each other in the direction of the offending contestant or contestants.
- To indicate cancelation of a wrongly awarded score, repeat the signal erroneously made with one hand while raising the other hand above the head to the front, waving it from right to left, two or three times. *Note:* If an amended score is to be awarded, it should be made soon as possible after this cancelation signal.
- To indicate the winner of the contest, raise the hand above shoulder height toward the winner.

The above signals are for the *referee only.* Judges' signals are as follows:

- To indicate that he considers a contes-

tant has stayed within the contest area, the judge shall raise one hand up in the air and bring it down to shoulder height along the boundary line of the contest area, generally with the thumb upward, and momentarily hold it there.
- To indicate that in his opinion one of the contestants is out of the contest area, the judge shall raise one hand to shoulder height along the boundary line of the contest area, generally with the thumb edge upward, and wave it from right to left several times.
- To indicate that in his opinion a score awarded by the referee, as in Article Twenty-Nine, has no validity whatsoever, the judge shall raise one of his hands above his head to the front and wave it from right to left, two or three times.
- To indicate a different opinion from the indicated motion of the referee, the judge shall make any of the signals a referee would to indicate his intention. It must conform to Article Twenty-Four.

ARTICLE THIRTY: PROHIBITED ACTS

All the following are prohibited acts.

I. Slight Infringements (penalized by *shido*)

1. To intentionally avoid taking hold of the opponent in order to prevent action in the contest.
2. To adopt an excessively defensive attitude.
3. To hold continually the opponent's collar, lapel, or sleeve on the same side with both hands or the opponent's belt or the bottom of his jacket with either or both hands.
4. To insert a finger or fingers inside the opponent's sleeve or the bottom of his pants or to grasp by "screwing action" the sleeve.
5. To stand continually with the fingers of one or both of his hands interlocked

in order to prevent action in the contest.

6. To intentionally disarrange his own *judogi* or to untie or retie the belt or the pants without the referee's permission.
7. To take hold of the opponent's leg or foot in order to change to *ne-waza*, unless exceptional skill is shown.
8. To wind the end of the belt or jacket around any part of opponent's body.
9. To take the opponent's *judogi* in the mouth or to put a hand or arm or foot or leg directly on the opponent's face.
10. To maintain (not let go) whilst lying on the back a hold with the legs round the neck or the armpit of the opponent when the opponent succeeds in standing or gets up to his knees in a position from which he could lift up the contestant.

II. Moderate Infringements (penalized by *chui*)

1. To apply action of *dojime* (leg scissors) to the opponent's trunk, neck, or head.
2. To kick with the knee or foot the hand or arm of the opponent in order to make him release his grasp.
3. To put a foot or leg in the opponent's belt, collar, or lapel or to bend back the opponent's finger or fingers in order to break the opponent's grip.
4. To pull the opponent down in order to start *ne-waza* (groundwork).

III. Serious Infringements (penalized by *keikoku*)

1. To intentionally force the opponent to go outside the contest area *for any reason* other than while applying a technique started in the contest area or except as a result of a technique or action of the opponent.
2. To attempt to throw the opponent with *kawazu-gake* (a throwing technique where you wind one leg around the opponent's leg whilst facing more or less in the same direction as opponent,

and falling backward on to him).

3. Applying *kansetsu-waza* on any joint other than the elbow.
4. To apply any action that might injure the neck or spinal vertebrae of the opponent.
5. To lift off the mat an opponent who is lying on his back in order to drive him back into the mat.
6. To sweep the opponent's supporting leg from the inside when the opponent is applying a technique such as *harai-goshi*.
7. To attempt to apply any technique outside the contest area.
8. To disregard the referee's instructions.
9. To make unnecessary calls, remarks, or gestures derogatory to the opponent during the contest.
10. To make any other action which may injure the opponent or may be against the spirit of judo.

IV. Very Serious Infringements (penalized by *hansoku-make*)

1. To intentionally fall backward when the other contestant is clinging to your back and when either contestant has control over the other's movement.

The above division of infringements into four groups is intended as a guide, to give a clearer understanding to all of the relative penalties normally awarded for committing the applicable prohibitory act. Referees and judges are authorized to award penalties according to the "intent" or "situation" and in the best interests of the sport.

Any contestant who performs or attempts any of the above acts shall be liable for disqualifications or other disciplinary action by the referee in accordance with these rules.

ARTICLE THIRTY-ONE: PENALTIES

The referee shall declare *shido* (note), *chui* (caution), *keikoku* (warning), or *hansoku-make* (disqualification) according to the severity of the infringements as outlined in Article Thirty.

If *shido* is announced to one contestant, the other shall be regarded as having scored *koka* (almost *yuko*); if *chui* is announced to one contestant, the other will be regarded as having scored *yuko* (almost *waza-ari*); if *keikoku* is awarded to a contestant, the other shall be regarded as having scored *waza-ari* (almost *ippon*).

Should the referee award *chui*, he shall temporarily stop the contest, return the contestants to a standing position in which they started the contest, and announce *chui* whilst raising his hand toward the contestant who committed the infringement.

Should the referee award *keikoku*, he shall temporarily stop the contest, return the contestants to start position, make them take a kneeling position, and announce *keikoku* while raising his hand toward the contestant who committed the infringement.

However, if the referee has called *osaekomi*, and it is the contestant being held down who commits the offense meriting a *keikoku*, then the referee shall call *sono-mama*, announce the *keikoku* in the *osaekomi* position, and then recommence the contest by calling *yoshi*.

Should the referee award *hansoku-made*, in accordance with rules and a discussion with the judges, he shall return the contestants back to start position, step between them, face the contestant in the wrong, point at him, and announce *hansoku-made*. He shall then step back to his original position and raise his hand to indicate the winner of the match.

Note: Penalties are noncumulative. Each penalty must be awarded on its own merit.

ARTICLE THIRTY-TWO: ASSESSMENT OF *IPPON* (FULL POINT)

The decision of *ippon* in a contest shall be given in the following cases:

A. Nage-Waza (throwing techniques)

1. When a clean throwing technique is applied and drops the opponent largely on his back with force and speed; when a counter-technique drops an opponent on his back with force and speed.

2. When a contestant skillfully lifts his opponent, who is lying on his back on the mat, up to about his shoulders.

B. Katame-Waza (grappling techniques)

1. When one contestant says *mai tai* (I surrender) or taps his opponent's body or the mat with his hand or foot twice or more.

2. When one contestant holds the other, on his back with control, for thirty seconds, after the announcement by the referee of *osaekomi*.

3. Where the effect of a technique of *shime-waza* (choking) or *kansetsu-waza* (arm locks) is sufficiently apparent.

ARTICLE THIRTY-THREE: ASSESSMENT OF *WAZA-ARI* (HALF POINT)

The decision of *waza-ari* shall be given in the following cases:

A. Nage-Waza

When a contestant applying a throw is not completely successful (e.g., the technique is lacking in one of three things: dropping opponent largely on back, force, or speed) and does not quite merit the score of *ippon*.

B. Katame-Waza

When one contestant holds an opponent in *osaekomi* (after referee announces it) for twenty-five seconds but less than thirty seconds.

ARTICLE THIRTY-FOUR: ASSESSMENT OF *YUKO*

The decision of *yuko* (almost *waza-ari*) shall be given in the following cases:

A. Nage-Waza

When a contestant applying a throwing technique is only partially successful. For example, is lacking more than is required to score *waza-ari*.

B. *Katame-Waza*

When an *osaekomi-waza* technique is effective for 20–25 seconds.

ARTICLE THIRTY-FIVE: ASSESSMENT OF *KOKA*

The decision of *koka* (almost *yuko*) shall be given in the following circumstances:

A. *Nage-Waza*

When a contestant makes a throwing technique which is not successful, but with some force of speed, puts his opponent on to his side, thigh, stomach, or buttocks and does not quite merit a score of *yuko*.

B. *Katame-Waza*

When an *osaekomi-waza* technique lasts for 10–20 seconds.

ARTICLE THIRTY-SIX: ASSESSMENT OF *YUSEI-GACHI*

The decision of *yusei-gachi* (superiority win) shall be generally given in the following cases:

1. Where there has been a score of *waza-ari* or a penalty of *keikoku*.
2. Where there has been a score of *yuko* or a penalty of *chui*.
3. Where there has been a score of *koka* or a penalty of *shido*.
4. Where all scores as recorded in Article Twenty-Five are equal for both contestants, the *yusei-gachi* shall be given to the contestant who has the least severe penalty recorded against him.
5. Where there is a recognizable difference in attitude during the contest or in the skill and effectiveness of the technique.

ARTICLE THIRTY-SEVEN: ASSESSMENT OF *HIKI-WAKE*

The decision of *hiki-wake* (draw) shall be given where there is no positive score and where it is impossible to judge the superiority of either contestant in accordance with Article Thirty-Six above within the time allotted for the contest.

ARTICLE THIRTY-EIGHT: ASSESSMENT OF *HANSOKU-MAKE*

The decision of *hansoku-make* (disqualification) should be given:

1. Where one contestant has had the penalty of *keikoku* awarded against him and then receives a further penalty.
2. Where any act on the part of one contestant gravely infringes Article Thirty above (Prohibited Acts) as, for example, where any act on his part may injure or endanger his opponent or any remark or gesture, etc., of his is considered to be contrary to the sport of judo.

ARTICLE THIRTY-NINE: DEFAULT AND WITHDRAWAL

The decision of *fusen-gachi* (win by default) shall be given to any contestant whose opponent does not appear for his contest.

The decision of *kiken-gachi* (win by withdrawal) shall be given to any contestant whose opponent withdraws from the competition during the contest.

ARTICLE FORTY: INJURY, ILLNESS, OR ACCIDENT

In every case where a competition is stopped because of injury to either or both of the contestants, the referee and judges may permit a maximum time of five minutes to the injured players for recuperation.

The decision of *kachi* (win), *make* (loss), or *hiki-wake* (draw), where one contestant is unable to continue because of injury, illness, or accident during the contest, shall be given by the referee, after consultation with judges, according to the following clauses:

A. Injury

1. Where the cause of the injury is attrib-

uted to the injured contestant, he shall lose the contest.

2. Where the cause of the injury is attributed to the uninjured contestant, the uninjured contestant shall lose the contest.

3. Where it is impossible to attribute the cause of the injury to either contestant, the decision of *hiki-wake* (draw) may be given.

B. Sickness

Generally, where one contestant is taken sick during a contest and is unable to continue, he shall lose the contest.

C. Accident

Where an accident occurs which is due to an outside influence, the decision of *hiki-wake* (draw) shall be given.

ARTICLE FORTY-ONE: SITUATIONS NOT COVERED BY THE RULES

Where any situation arises which is not covered by these rules, it shall be dealt with and a decision given by the referee after consultation with the judges.

APPENDIX IV:
THE KATA OF JUDO

Like other martial arts, such as karate and kung fu, judo has its own set of *kata* (forms). The *kata* are prearranged movements enacted by two individuals to a formal, set routine. Each movement must be exact and executed in a specific manner. The reasons for *kata* are many and varied, and a full discussion on them is beyond the scope of this particular text, as is an actual photo demonstration of each technique of each *kata*.

However, *kata* do fulfill a very important part of judo, as an art and a cultural activity. Because of the difficulty of mastery and the rigid standards, *kata* can be called a true art form, adding a dimension to judo not ordinarily understood by sportsmen alone.

In addition to the aesthetic qualities of *kata*, form training has a very practical and somewhat secret side. The *kata* in essence preserve the actual concepts and techniques of classical judo. They are also said to hold the secrets of the ancient masters. In reality *kata* preserve antiquity.

Last, by mastering some *kata* like the *goshin-jutsu* form, one learns very practical self-

defense methods that can be applied directly to the street.

The following is a brief explanation of the major judo *kata* in use by the *kodokan* today.

NAGE-NO-KATA (FORMS OF THROWING)

Invented in 1890 by Dr. Kano, this kata consists of 15 throwing techniques broken down into five categories: *te-waza* (hand techniques), *koshi-waza* (hip techniques), *ashi-waza* (leg techniques), *ma-sutemi-waza* (rear sacrificing throws), and *yoko-sutemi-waza* (side sacrificing throws).

Dr. Kano selected the most representative throws from each of the five categories to show the wide range of throwing actions used in judo.

KATAME-NO-KATA (FORMS OF HOLDING)

Invented by Dr. Kano around 1893, this too consists of 15 techniques broken down into three categories (5 techniques per category): *osae-komi-waza* (holding/pinning techniques), *shime-waza* (choking techniques), and *kansetsu-waza* (joint locks).

The criteria for each group are different from those in *nage-no-kata*. The only concern is with type of technique, not with application of technical factors at all; therefore, many feel that it is superficial and does not have any value.

However, the kata do contain much *reishiki* and as such have value in the realm of art and ritual.

KIME-NO-KATA (FORMS OF DECISION *OR* FORMS OF SELF-DEFENSE)

Applying techniques of throwing and grappling to which body attack techniques are added, *kime-no-kata* are intended to form the most basic and effective way of defending oneself from unexpected attacks.

Kime-no-kata are composed of 8 techniques from a kneeling posture (*idori*), and 12 techniques from a standing position (*tachiai*).

The practice of *kime-no-kata* will teach the principles of defense and counterattack along with manipulative body movements.

KODOKAN GOSHIN-JUTSU (SELF-DEFENSE TECHNIQUES) OF KODOKAN JUDO

This *kata* is a new form of *kime-no-kata* invented by the Kodokan Institute in 1956 after three years of tireless contemplation. It consists of 21 techniques suitable for defending oneself from unexpected attacks.

The nature of these 21 techniques is similar to the 20 techniques of *kime-no-kata*; however, the substance and practicing methods of these techniques are devoid of *reishiki* and ritual, making this a very practical *kata*.

KOSHIKI-NO-KATA (FORMS OF ANTIQUITY)

This *kata* actually *preserves* the secrets of the old *kito-ryu jujutsu* school. Very rarely seen

(because very few know the *kata*), it includes 21 attacks plus responses to the front, and 7 to the back. This is a very classical *kata* that one requires a lifetime of study to truly appreciate.

ITSUSU-NO-KATA (FORMS OF FIVE)

This *kata* was never finished by Dr. Kano, but it was intended to be his masterpiece. It was to contain the complete concepts of *ju* and *tai-sabaki*.

It is an attempt to show, in physical rhythmic patterns, the play of forces in a cosmological combat situation; that is, Kano was trying to show that the microcosmic forces contained in human confrontation are essentially the same as those macrocosmic forces contained in the creation of the universe.

JU-NO-KATA (FORMS OF GENTLENESS)

A sequence of 15 movements (some done up to the point of throwing action and then the opponent is placed down) divided into three *kyos* (sets). The object is to show how the principle of *ju* can manifest itself in different ways in different situations.

JOSHI JUDO GOSHIHO (KODOKAN SELF-DEFENSE TECHNIQUES FOR WOMEN)

This kata was invented by the *kodokan* in order to take the best advantage of a woman's body structure and physical characteristics. It is a complete study of body movement, *atemi-waza* (striking/kicking), and escape tactics from holds.

SEIRYOKU-ZENYO KOKUMIN-TAIIKU (NATIONAL PHYSICAL EXERCISE BASED ON THE PRINCIPLE OF MAXIMUM EFFICIENCY)

This exercise is aimed at developing all muscles of your body in proper harmony and also increase harmonious strength. It consists of 28 or 16 individual exercises in *tai-sabaki* and *atemi-waza* (the number of techniques depends on how you are counting them). There are also 10 pair exercises against body attacks with and without weapons.

The *kata* is a product of 1880, and many of the techniques reflect this antiquity.

RENKOHO-NO-KATA (FORMS OF ARREST *OR* FORMS OF RESTRAINT)

A very short *kata* illustrating very practical techniques of control, which are used exclusively by the Japanese Police as come-along and arrest holds.

KIME-SHIKI (FORMS OF DECISION)

This exercise aims to build your body properly by developing muscles that result in fast and graceful movements of your whole body. Further, it is considerably effective at teaching body movements essential in life-or-death situations. The *kata* consists of five techniques kneeling (*idori*), and five techniques standing (*tachiai*). A very ritualistic yet extremely practical and effective *kata*.

APPENDIX V:
GLOSSARY

Aiki-Jutsu: Translates as the "art of inner harmony." A warrior method of striking, kicking, and joint manipulation. Techniques are the same as in modern-day *aikido;* however, they are much more brutal. *Aiki-jutsu* also uses weapons such as the sword and staff.

Aikido: Translates as the "way of spiritual harmony." An art that manipulates an opponent's oncoming force, turning it against the attacker, and either immobilizing him or projecting (throwing) him. This is accomplished through intricate body movement and joint manipulation. The goal of *aikido* is harmony with an attacker; it is a passive, nonaggressive art. The refined form of *aiki-jutsu.*

Ago: Chin.

Aite: Partner, attacker, or opponent.

Aka: Red.

Antei: Stability, in reference to posture.

Arashi: Storm (as in *arashi-gaeshi,* the "storm throw").

Ashi-Kubi: Ankle.

Ashi-Waza: Leg techniques (referring to throws and holds.

Atama: Head.

Ate: To strike.

Ate-Waza: Striking techniques.

Atemi: To hit.

Atemi-Waza: The branch of judo dealing with punching, striking, and kicking techniques.

Awase Waza: Two half-points in competition.

Bakufu: Refers to the military government of Japan during the years 1603–1868. A time that warrior arts became arts of peace.

Bakumatsu: The fall of the *bakufu* government. Brought about the Meiji Restoration in the 1800s.

Barai: Sweep (ancient).

Budo: The martial ways. These are refined arts from a warrior heritage, such as judo from *jujutsu,* or *kendo* from *ken-jutsu. Budo* can be identified by the *do* (way) suffix at the end of a martial way (such as ju*do,* and ken*do*).

Bu-Jutsu: Martial arts or military arts. Can be identified by the *jutsu* suffix at the end of a word (e.g., ju*jutsu* or aiki-*jutsu*). These are the combat alternatives to *budo.*

Bushido: The samurai's code of ethics. Translates as "way of the warrior." The code was formalized by the samurai Yoku Yamagei.

Butsukari: In judo practice, technique of movement or *tsukuri* for a technique, preceding *kake* (execution). See **Kake** and **Uchikomi**.

Chairo: Brown (color).

Chi: An intrinsic life force that is stored in the *tantien* (located three inches below the navel). It can be either flowing in the body (called *jun chi*), as in acupuncture, or outside the body, as the force that makes all life possible (called *wei chi*).

Chikara: Physical strength.

Chui: Attention.

Chui Nikai: A second warning in a contest.

Chui-Ikkai: A first warning in a competition.

Daimyos: Territory leaders in feudal Japan.

Dan: Translates as "graded." This is a graduate of the judo system. The belts worn in *dan* are black, red and white, and red.

Deshi: Student.

Dho: Trunk of the body.

Dojo: Place of practice; the judo hall or gym. Word connotes great respect.

Eri: Collar on the judo uniform (*gi*).

Fukkaysu: Term refers to reviving an unconscious choking victim in a judo contest.

Fukoku-Kyohei: Refers to Japan's hope of achieving world recognition during the Meiji Restoration.

Fuku Shiki Kokyu: Deep breathing, to catch breath.

Fusegi: Defense.

Fusen Gachi: Winner by forfeit.

Fusensho: To win by default.

Gambaru: To stiffen up; to resist a throw.

Gari: A very powerful sweeping or "reaping" action in throwing techniques.

Genki: To be "psyched up" for a match. Also refers to energy and/or vitality.

Genshin: The ability to anticipate an opponent's movement before the movement occurs.

Gokyo-Waza: Forms of five throws (sets). Eight throws per five sets, totaling 40 techniques. In many schools the accomplishment of technical proficiency per set can raise an individual in rank. This is not universally practiced as a means of promotion.

Goshin: Self-defense.

Guruma: Wheel action in throwing techniques.

Gyaku: Reverse action.

Gyaku Ni Motsu: Holding an opponent's lapel with fingers on the inside and thumbs on the outside.

Hadaka: Naked (as in choking).

Hakama: A traditional skirt worn in judo and *aikido* (sometimes *jujutsu*).

Hakuda: Another term for *jujutsu*.

Hana: Nose.

Hanasu: To release one's grip.

Hane: Spring (as a throwing action).

Hansoku: Rules and regulations.

Hansoku Gachi: Winner by violation.

Hansoku Make: To lose a match by violation of rules.

Hantei: Decision or judgment (in a match).

Hajime: To start or begin.

Harai: A sweeping action in a throw.

Hara: The center of the body (three inches below the navel). Also refers to centering, the act of movement from the center of the body in contrast to using arm or leg strength alone.

Happo-No-Kuzushi: The eight directions of off-balancing an opponent.

Hidari: Left.

Hiji: Elbow.

Hineru: To twist sharply, as in *uki-goshi*.

Hiza: Knee.

Hiza Gashira: Kneecap.

Hoko: Direction.

Holistic Judo: A term used to refer to a complete system of judo in which *all* judo values are stressed, not just contest skill.

Iai-Do: The art of drawing the sword. A classical *budo* art.

Ibuki: Tension breathing used to develop strength.

Ippo: One step.

Ippon: One point (in competition).

Itsusu-No-Kata: Forms of five. An advanced judo *kata*.

Jibun: Self, in contrast to opponent.

Jigohontai (or Jigotai): Self-defense posture.

Jikan: Time (command of referee).

Jiki: Axis, pivot, used in *tsukuri* (also called *jiku*).

Jikishin-Ryu: The first *jujutsu* school to use the term *judo*. However, it did not become popular until Dr. Kano used it.

Jime: To squeeze (choking action).

Jishin: Self-confidence.

Jo: Staff, four feet long.

Ju: The concept of gentleness fundamental to judo and *jujutsu*. Also translated as "yielding."

Judo: "The gentle way." Invented by Dr. Jigoro Kano in 1882, it is a *do* form of *jujutsu*, with emphasis placed on development of the entire person.

Judogi: Judo uniform.

Judoka: Person who practices judo.

Jo-Gai: Outside.

Joshi Judo Goshiho: A judo *kata*. Translates as "The *Kodokan*'s self-defense for women."

Juji: Cross.

Jujutsu: An ancient self-defense art that used throwing, grappling, striking, and kicking. It also employed a number of weapons. The samurai relied on *jujutsu* when he was without his swords. Being a *jutsu* art, it relies on practical combat instead of personal perfection as do *do* arts.

Jun Ni Motsu: To hold an opponent's *gi* with the fingers on the outside and the thumb on the inside.

Ju No Kata: A judo *kata*. Translates as the "forms of gentleness."

Jushin: Balance.

Jushin No Ushinau: To lose one's balance.

Kaeshiwaza: Countertechniques in judo.

Kaiden: "Everything passed." Refers to an ancient *bu-jutsu* grading system used today only in *aiki-jutsu* and some *jujutsu* schools. Equivalent to eighth- to tenth-degree black belt ranks in use in modern judo.

Kake: The actual execution of the throwing action of a technique. The last stage.

Kano, Jigoro: The founder of judo.

Karate: "The empty hand." Refers to the art of striking, kicking, punching, and blocking as practiced in Japan and Okinawa. The major Okinawan styles are: *goju-ryu, shorin-ryu, shorei-ryu, uechi-ryu, isshin-ryu,* etc. The major Japanese styles are: *goju-ryu, shito-ryu, shoto-kan, wado-ryu, kyokushinkai-kan, rembukai,* etc.

Kappo: The art of reviving an unconscious person. Also an intricate form of Japanese first aid required for promotion to black belt in some systems.

Kansetsu: Manipulation of the joints to cause pain and/or dislocation.

Karada: Body.

Karami: To coil (an action of a throw).

Kata: (1) Shoulder; (2) Stylized formal practice where each movement is prearranged, in contrast to *randori* training.

Katame-No-Kata: A judo *kata*. Translates as "forms of holding."

Katame Waza: Holding techniques. Divided into *osaekomi-waza* (pinning), *shime-waza* (choking), and *kansetsu-waza* (joint techniques).

Kega: Injury.

Keiko: Workout or practice session.

Keikobo: Severe violation of the rules.

Keikoku: Severe warning.

Kempo: The Japanese word for *kung fu* (Chinese). Some people use the term interchangeably with *jujutsu*.

Kengaku: Instruction by observation: to watch one perform as a means of instruction.

Kesa: Scarf (as in holding).

Ki: Spirit or energy. See **Chi**.

Kiai: Shout.

Kime: (1) Focusing strength on a single point; (2) the finishing technique in self-defense.

Kime-No-Kata: A judo *kata*. Translates as "forms of self-defense."

Kime-Shiki: A judo *kata*. Translates as "forms of decision."

Kito-Ryu: A style of *jujutsu* Dr. Kano studied to form judo. He studied it under the eye of Iikudo Tsunetoshi. *Kito-ryu* is noted for its throwing techniques and its hard but effective self-defense techniques.

Kinsa: Small advantage.

Ko: Minor, small, lesser.

Kodokan: (1) The school or *dojo* Kano established to teach his judo. It is now the world headquarters for judo. (2) The name of Kano's judo style (*kodokan* judo), founded in 1882.

Kodokan Goshin-Jutsu: A judo *kata*. Translates as "the *kodokan's* method of self-defense." A very practical *kata*.

Koshi: Hip (throwing action).

Koshiki-No-Kata: A judo *kata*. Translates as "forms of antiquity." It holds the secrets of the *kito-ryu* style of *jujutsu*. A very ritualistic *kata*.

Kotai: To retreat.

Kubi: Neck (throwing action).

Kuchi: Mouth.

Kumikata: Holding techniques. Also refers to the beginning posture, where one grasps the other's uniform. Methods of gripping the uniform.

Kumiuchi: Another term for *jujutsu*.

Kung Fu: Chinese form of karate. More ritualistic.

Kuzushi: The act of breaking an opponent's balance. A preliminary movement in a throwing action.

Kyogi/Kogi: Refers to the three cultural principles of judo established by Dr. Kano to be the higher values of his art. *Kyogi* are the lesser values (contest, physical fitness); *kogi* are the greater values (mental cultivation, attitude, and character).

Ma: Direct.

Mae: Front.

Mae-Waza: Forward techniques.

Makkikomi: Wind in (a throwing action where one loses his balance to draw the other down).

Ma Sutemi Waza: Techniques of throwing an opponent when you fall to your *rear* to take him with you.

Mata: Thigh.

Mawashi: To turn.

Ma Yoko: Directly to the side.

Meiji Restoration: A time in Japanese history when the *shogun* lost his power by returning it to the emperor (*meiji*). This brought a time in Japanese history when martial arts had to adapt or disappear. Judo was born during this era.

Menkyo: An ancient ranking designation. Translates as "licensed." Equivalent to fourth- to seventh-degree black belt.

Migi: Right.

Mochikata: The methods of gripping an opponent's *gi*. Sometimes called *kumikata* instead. *Mochikata* are broken down into A, B, and C grips.

Moku-Roku: An ancient ranking designation. Translates as "cataloged." Equivalent to third- to fourth-degree black belts.

Mudansha: One without grade. It is used to designate all ranks under black belt.

Muri Ni: To attempt to move in vain as with strength in contrast to judo principles.

Mushin: Zen concept of "no mind," that is, keeping the mind empty so it can reflect on all that is around it without thoughts and intellect interfering with genuine perception.

Mushin-No-Shin: Translates as "mind of no mind." See **Mushin**.

Nage: To throw.

Nage-No-Kata: A judo *kata*. Translates as "forms of throwing." The first and most popular judo *kata* learned.

Nage-Waza: Throwing techniques.

Ne-Waza: Techniques performed from a lying position. Can be *nage-waza* or *katame-waza*.

Niho: Two steps.

Nodo: Throat.

Nogare: A breathing exercise that is most natural and applicable to the breathing used in the execution of techniques.

Nogarekata: Methods of escaping from an opponent's techniques.

O: Major.

Obi: Belt.

Oku-Eri: An ancient rank designation used today by *jujutsu* and *aiki-jutsu* schools. Equivalent to first-degree black belt. Translates as "entrance to secrets."

Okuri: Send off (a throwing action).

Okyu Teate: First aid.

Osaekomi Toketa: A term used in competition to refer to the fact that a hold-down has been broken.

Osaekomi Waza: Holding and pinning techniques.

Oshi: Push (a throwing action).

Otoshi: Drop (a throwing action).

Prana: A yogic word referring to the force of life. See also **Chi, Ki**.

Pranayama: Yogic breathing exercises.

Randori: Free play, or free fighting.

Randori-No-Kata: Basic forms of *randori* (*nage-no-kata* and *katame-no-kata*).

Rei: To bow.

Reigisaho: Physical development (an aim of judo).

Reishiki: Etiquette, ritual, stylistic practices.

Renkoho-No-Kata: A judo *kata*. Translates as "forms of arrest." A kata consisting of come-along holds and arresting methods.

Renshiho: Proper manners, correct conduct on the mat.

Rentai-Ho: One of the three cultural principles of judo. It is part of *kyogi* (narrow aims). It refers to physical fitness.

Renshu: Practice.

Renraku Waza: Continuation technique, as from one technique to another. Also refers to alternate (backup) throwing techniques.

Ritsu Rei: Standing bow.

Ryu: A term used as a suffix to ancient styles of combat. Translates as "school."

Saikatanden: See Hara.

Sampo: Three steps.

Sasae: Check, prop, hold back (a throwing action).

Seigo-Ryu: A style of *jujutsu* Dr. Kano studied in his latter development. It played a lesser role in judo than did *kito-ryu* and *tenshin shinyo-ryu*.

Seiryo-Zenyo: Translates as the "best use of energy." It is also the key to all judo techniques. Sometimes translated as "maximum efficiency with minimum effort."

Seiryoku-Zenyo Komumin-Taiiku: A judo *kata*. Translates as "national physical exercise based on maximum efficiency."

Seiza: Kneeling position.

Sekiguchi-Ryu: A *jujutsu* style Dr. Kano studied that played a lesser part in judo's development.

Semeru: To attack.

Sensei: Teacher.

Sessei: Care of health.

Seoi: Upper back region (a throwing action).

Senaka: Lower back region.

Shiai: Match, contest, tournament.

Shiaijo: Tournament mat area.

Shido: Small infraction of the rules.

Shintai: Advance/retreat. A fundamental beginning to any throwing action.

Shihan: Master teacher.

Shime Waza: Choking techniques. A part of *katame-waza*.

Shiroi: White (color).

Shita: Down below (a throwing action).

Shitagi: The pants of a *judogi*.

Shitsu Kansetsu: Knee joint.

Shisei: Posture.

Shizentai: Natural standing posture.

Shobu: Match, bout.

Shobu-Ho: One of the three cultural principles. Part of the *kyogi* (lesser aims). Refers to being expert at contest skills.

Shomen: Refers to judo rank of a child 13–17 years of age. A teenage rank between child (*yonen*) and senior.

Shubaku: Another term for *jujutsu*.

Sosai: Equivalent.

Soto: Outside (a throwing action).

Suigetsu: Mid-chest (solar plexus).

Sumi: Corner (throwing/holding direction).

Sushin-Ho: Part of the three cultural principles of judo. Part of the *koji* (higher values). Refers to mental cultivation.

Sutemi: Sacrificing throws.

Susumeru: To advance.

Suti: A classification of two very important commands in judo: (1) *Sono Mama:* to freeze. A command given during a contest where the referee wants the action stopped, but the positions held. (2) *Soremade:* end of match.

Tachi Gyaku: Techniques of *kansetsu waza* applied while standing up.

Tachi Waza: Techniques performed standing up, in contrast to *ne waza*.

Tachirei: Standing bow.

Tai: Body (throwing action).

Tai Chi Chaun: A Chinese form of *kung fu*. Very soft, slow, and graceful. Very effective.

Tai Jutsu: Used to imply body techniques (also another word for *jujutsu).*

Taisabaki: Body shifting. A preliminary to throwing.

Tan Doku Keiko: Solo practice.

Tani: Valley (a throwing description).

Takenouchi-Ryu: One of the first recorded systems of *jujutsu.* Founded in 1532 by Takenouchi Hisamori.

Tao-Te-Ching: A great book in Chinese Taoism, authored by Lao-tzu.

Tatami: Mat.

Te: Hand.

Te Kubi: Wrist.

Te Waza: Hand techniques (usually referring to hand throws).

Tenshin-Shinyo-Ryu: One of the main styles of *jujutsu* Dr. Kano studied to form judo. It stresses grappling and *aikido*-like throwing techniques. A form of *aiki-jutsu.*

Toketa: To break a hold.

Tomoe: Whirl (a throwing action).

Tori: The executor of an action. The thrower.

Torite: Another word for *jujutsu.*

Tsukuri: A fitting action prior to execution of a technique. Attack preparation.

Tsume: Fingernails or toenails.

Tsuri: Lift (throwing action).

Tsuri-Komi: Lift-pull (a throwing action).

Uchi: Inner (a throwing action).

Uchikomi: Practice of techniques of throwing by having your *uke* (receiver) stand still while you lift him up and practice the *tsukuri,* but holding off on the *kake.*

Ude: Forearm.

Uke: Receiver of a technique (the "throwee").

Ukemi: Breakfalls.

Uki: Float (a throwing action).

Undo: Conditioning exercises.

Ura: Reverse (a throwing action).

Ushiro: Back (a throwing action).

Utsuri: Change (a throwing action).

Uwagi: The jacket of a *judogi.*

Wa-Jutsu: Another term for *jujutsu.*

Waza: Technique (suffix).

Waza-Ari: Half-point.

Waza-Ari Awasete Ippon: Two half-points equal one point.

Wushu: Another term for Chinese karate (*kung fu*).

Yama-Ji: "Mountain temple." The school established by Sensei George R. Parulski, Jr. (author), in 1970. Stresses higher values of most traditional *budo* and *bu-jutsu.*

Yang: See **Yin/Yang.**

Yawara: Another term for *jujutsu.*

Yin/Yang: The Chinese taoist concept of opposites. Yang represents male, positive elements of universe; yin represents female, negative principles of universe.

Yoko: Side (a throwing action).

Yoko Sutemi Waza: Side sacrificing throws where *tori* falls to his side to drag *uke* down.

Yonen: A child's rank in judo; 12 years of age and under.

Yoshi: A right. A contest yell.

Yudansha: Graded student. Refers to black belt and higher rank.

Yuseigachi: To win a match by superiority as seen by judges.

Zabaki: Walking procedures in judo.

Zarei: Kneeling bow.

Zempo Ukemi: Rolling (forward) breakfalls.

Zanshin: Fighting spirit.

Zen: A philosophy brought from India to China in 520 A.D. by Bodhidharma. There are three main sects: Soto, Rinzai, and Obato. Zen mixed with all fighting arts during the *bakufu* to make them arts of peace and cultivation. See **Mushin.**

JAPANESE COUNTING

Ik—one
Ni—two
San—three
Yo or *Yon*—four
Go—five
Roku—six
Shichi—seven
Hachi—eight
Ku—nine
Ju—ten

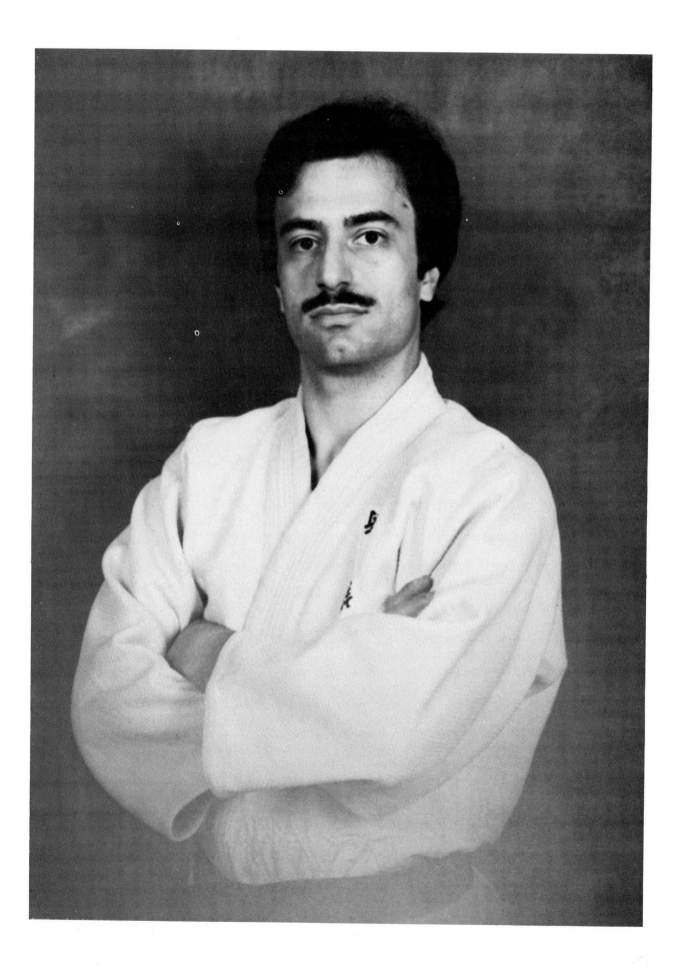

ABOUT THE AUTHOR

A member of the prestigious American Society of Classical Judoka, George R. Parulski, Jr., has compiled a brilliant record of achievement in the martial arts. Born in Rochester, New York, in 1954, he has become one of America's top martial arts writers and practitioners, with black belt rankings in several traditional and modern martial ways (*budo*).

Beginning in 1963, at the age of eight, he had his first lessons with James D. Mounts and Frank L. Lane (the latter awarded him his first black belt ranking).

As a competitor, Parulski was very active in both judo and karate, winning more than 50 tournaments. His most prestigious titles include 1974 East Coast Judo Championships (first place, Open Weight) and 1983 American Karate Federation's Grand Nationals (Grand Champion, Master Kata division; first place, Black Belt Weapons).

Parulski holds a yondan (fourth-degree black belt) in judo, fourth-degree black belt in *shotokan* karate (American Karate Federation), first-degree black belt in *iai-do* (sword drawing), first-degree black belt in *aikido (Dai-Nippon Seibukan Budo/Bugei Kai), menkyo* in *tenshin-shinyo-ryu aiki-jujutsu (Dai-Nippon Seibukan Budo/Bugei Kai)*, and white sash in *Tai Chi Ch'uan kung fu* and Northern/Southern *Shaolin* (Chinese Wu-Shu Federation). In addition, he was accepted into the Eisho-ji Zen Community (Corning, New York), where he lived for three summers, enhancing his philosophical background in martial arts. Parulski studied in Asian Studies at St. John Fisher College.

Aside from Parulski's vast knowledge of martial arts, those who were competing in the '60s on the East Coast will remember him for his remarkable sword demonstrations. Parulski feels the sword, of all martial arts weapons, holds the true spirit of *bushido* (way of the warrior) and that perfection of the sword brings about perfection of the mind.

Currently, Parulski is devoting most of his energies to the formation of the Yama-ji: School of Traditional Martial Arts. The Yama-ji (mountain temple) is not a temple in the architectural sense but in the metaphysical sense. The student of *budo* beginning his training is compared with a traveler walking up the mountainside to the temple in the clouds. With each step he takes (each belt advancement), he sees the view a bit more clearly but realizes there is still a better view of the temple above. When he reaches the temple (the black belt) and looks up into the clouds he realizes there is still a higher place, and no matter how much he learns there will always be more ahead.

Parulski is the author of *A Path to Oriental Wisdom* (Ohara Publications) and is a regular contributor to *Black Belt, Karate Illustrated, Official Karate, Warriors, Muscle-up, Bodybuilder,* and *Police Product News.*

He makes his home in Webster, New York, with his wife, Carolyn, daughter Jackie, and son Charlie.

ABOUT THE ASSISTANTS

ROB HOROWITZ

Born in Rochester, New York, Horowitz, 25, holds certification in both judo and *aiki-jutsu*. Schooled at Duke University (Durham, North Carolina) and St. John Fisher College (Rochester, New York), Rob works full-time as a crisis interventionist counselor with emotionally disturbed children at Hillside Children's Center. In his spare time he considers himself a "recluse," preferring such solitary activities as reading, writing, drawing, playing music (piano, trumpet, bass), running, and camping. "Perhaps this influenced my early involvement in martial arts," speculates Horowitz. "I have always been interested in the gentleness and primary defensive nature of judo, *jujutsu*, and *aiki-jutsu (aikido)*. My desire to study these in a manner that embraced not just the physical aspects, but the philosophy, spirituality, and history that form their basis, was fulfilled when I met Sensei Parulski."

Rob resides in Rochester, New York, and is the coordinator of activities for Yama-ji.

BILL ROURKE

W. P. (Bill) Rourke was born in Brantford, Ontario, Canada, on August 27, 1942. Educated in Rochester, New York, Rourke holds a bachelor of science degree in industrial marketing from the Rochester Institute of Technology.

In addition to holding certification in judo and *aiki-jutsu*, Rourke was a wrestling champion in Long Island, New York, and in Toronto, Ontario, Canada.

Rourke's greatest asset in judo is his ability to counter his opponent's oncoming attack. He also has very powerful *ashi-waza* (leg techniques), which he uses successfully both offensively and defensively.

He gratefully expresses his thanks to his wife Pat and daughters Ashley and Brooke for their sacrifices and understanding while he pursues the teachings of the gentle art of judo.

END NOTES

CHAPTER 1: HISTORICAL BACKGROUND

1. Donn Draeger, *Modern Bu-jutsu and Budo* (Tokyo, Japan: Weatherhill, Inc., 1974), p. 112.

2. Ibid., p. 19.

3. Ibid., p. 18.

4. Kodokan, *Illustrated Kodokan Judo* (Japan: Kodansha International, 1970), p. 1.

5. Draeger, *Modern Bu-jutsu and Budo*, p. 113.

6. Hayward Nishioka, *Judo Textbook* (Burbank, California: Ohara Publications, Inc., 1979), p. 180.

7. Ibid, p. 181.

8. *Modern Bu-Jutsu and Budo*, p. 115.

9. *Illustrated Kodokan Judo*, p. 9.

10. *Judo Textbook*, p. 182.

CHAPTER 2: THEORY

1. *Illustrated Kodokan Judo*, p. 20.

2. *Modern Bu-Jutsu and Budo*, p. 118.

3. Dave Lowry, "Reishiki," *Karate Illustrated Magazine* (August 1983), p. 66.

4. Ibid., p. 67.

5. Kudo, *Judo-in-Action: Vol. #1 Throwing Techniques* (Japan Publications, Inc., 1967), p. 12.

6. Watanabe, *Secrets of Judo* (Tokyo, Japan: Tuttle Company, 1963), p. 35.

7. Ibid., p. 37.

8. *Judo-in-Action*, p. 11.

BIBLIOGRAPHY

Draeger, Donn F. *Asian Fighting Arts.* Tokyo, Japan: Kodansha International, 1978.

———. *Classical Bu-jutsu.* Tokyo, Japan: Weatherhill, 1973.

———. *Classical Budo.* Tokyo, Japan: Weatherhill, 1974.

———. *Modern Bu-jutsu and Budo.* Tokyo, Japan: Weatherhill, 1975.

Geesink, Anton. *Gokyo-waza.* New York: Arco Publishing Co., 1963.

———. *My Championship Judo.* New York: Arco Publishing Co., Inc., 1964.

Kodokan. *Illustrated Kodokan Judo.* Japan: Kodansha International, 1970.

Kudo, Kazuzo. *Judo-in-Action, Vol. One: Throwing Techniques.* Tokyo, Japan: Japan Publications, Inc., 1967.

———. *Judo-in-Action. Vol. Two: Grappling Techniques.* Tokyo, Japan: Japan Publications, Inc., 1963.

Lowry, Dave. "Reishiki" *(Karate Illustrated Magazine).* Rainbow Publications, Inc., August, 1983.

Nishioka, Hayward. *The Judo Textbook.* Burbank, California: Ohara Publications, Inc., 1979.

Parulski, George. *A Path to Oriental Wisdom.* Burbank, California: Ohara Publications, Inc., 1976.

Watanabe. *Secrets of Judo.* Tokyo, Japan: Charles Tuttle Co., Inc., 1963.

INDEX

Aikido, 3, 8, 43
Alternate breathing, 44–45
American Society of Classical Judoka, 5, 9
Amino acids (proteins), 147–48
Ankle Pops (exercises), 50–51
Asahi Prize, 4
Asana (yoga postures), 23, 24–42
Ashi-guruma (Leg Wheel Throw), 95–95
Ate-waza, 3
Atemi, 3, 117

Bakufu (military government), 1
Bakumatsu, 1
Balance, 15–19
Batsugun (superior player), 146
Bee pollen, 153
Belt exercises, 54–56
Belts, 12, 13
   ranking, 143–46
Body, 17, 23–24, 141
Bow. *See Rei*
Bow and Arrow Pose (yoga), 32–33
Breakfall techniques. *See Ukemi-waza*
Breathing exercises, 46–48
Budo (martial ways), 1, 2
Bu-jutsu, 2, 9

Caffeine, 153
Calcium, 149
Candle Pose (yoga), 34–35
Carbohydrates, 148
Centering, 15, 17, 19, 67
Character, 141

Charter Oath, 2
Chest breathing, 43
Chi (intrinsic energy), 43
Child Pose (yoga), 41
Chlorine, 149
Cholesterol, 152
Cleanliness, 25
Complete breathing (yoga), 44
Conditioning exercises, 48–57
Coordination, 17–18
Cow Pose (yoga) 36–38

Daimyos (Land Leaders), 1
"Dai Nippon kodokan judo" (expression: "Best judo in all
   Japan"), 8
Dai-Nippon Seibukan Judo-Kai (All Japan Seibukan
   Judo Association), x, 5
De-Ashi Barai (Drawing Ankle Sweep Throw), 68–70
Do (way), 3
Dojo (gym), 9, 12, 14, 25

Eishoi-ji, school of Zen, 23
Etiquette. *See Reishiki*
Emotional control, 24
Endorphin (body drug), 24
Extension Posture (yoga), 34–36

Fats, 148
Fish Pose (yoga), 30–31
Food, 25
Force, use of, 15–16
"Fukoku-kyohei" (expression: "Build a strong nation"), 2

Geesink, Anton, 135
Gentleness. *See Ju*
Gi (judo uniform), 12–13, 154, 159
Goals, 135–136
Gokyo-waza (Throwing Forms of Five), 67–68
Grounded, 15, 67
Gyaku juju-jime (Reverse Strangle Hold), 128–29

Hadaka-jime (Naked Choke), 128–29
Hakama (skirt), 9
Hakuda, 2
Handstand, 36–37
Hane-goshi (Spring Hip Throw), 94–95
Hane Maki-komi (Spring Wrapping Throw), 100, 102–3, 106
Hantei (decision in contest), 159
Happo-no-kuzushi, 17–19
Hara (center), 15
Harai-goshi (Sweeping Hip Throw), 88–89, 94, 104
Harai Tsuri-komi-ashi (Sweeping Pulling Ankle Throw), 96–97
Headstand, 25–27
Herbs, 133
High breathing, 43
Hiza Gatame (Knee Lock), 124–25
Hiza Guruma (Knee Wheel Throw), 70–71, 72
Holistic conditioning, 22–65
Holistic judo, 2
Honey, 24, 152, 153
Hurdler Stretch (exercise), 52–53
Hygiene, 12, 14

Ibuki breathing, 46–47
Integration, 23–24, 137
Intellect, 141
International Judo Federation, 5
Internation Olympic Council, 4
Ippon (full-point), 157, 158
Ippion Seoinage (One-Arm Over Shoulder Throw). *See Seoinage*
Iron, 150
Isometric exercises, 56–57
Itsusu-no-kata (judo kata), 165

Jigotai, 19–21
Jikishin-ryu (jujutsu system), 2, 4
Jo (4-foot staff), 3
Joshi judo goshin (kodokan self-defense for women), 166
Ju (gentleness), 7, 8, 19, 106, 108, 114, 165
Judo Medical Research Society, 3
Juji Gatame (Cross Arm Lock), 124–25
Jujutsu, 2, 3, 4, 8, 12, 98, 144
Ju-no-kata (forms of gentleness), 165
Jutsu (art), 4
"*Ju yoko go o sei suru*" (expression: Softness controls hardness; weakness controls strength), 7

Kaiden, 143
Kake (execution of throw), 14, 19
Kami Shiho Gatame (Upper Four Corners Hold), 118–19, 120–21
Kano, Jigoro (1860–1938), x, 2, 3–4, 7, 8, 9, 12, 77, 98, 141, 144, 168
Kansetsu-waza (locking techniques), 117, 120–27, 165
"*Karada o shite seishin ni jujun narashimeru jutsu*" (expression: Making the body obedient to the mind), 8
Kata (form), 12, 144, 164–66
Kata Gatame (Shoulder Hold), 118–19
Kata Guruma (Shoulder Wheel Throw), 98–99
Kata-ha Jime (Cross Choking Hold), 128–31
Kata juji-jime, 126–29
Katame-no-kata (forms of holding), 165
Katame-waza (holding techniques), 3, 116–33, 161, 162
Kempo, 2
Ken-jutsu (sword fighting), 8
Kesa Gatame (Scarf Hold), 118–19
Ketosis (disease), 148
Ki (spirit), 43
Kiai (shouting), 46, 48
Kime-no-kata (forms of self-defense), 165
Kime-shiki (forms of decision), 166
Kito-ryu (jujutsu school), 7, 8, 16
Knee Rotations (exercise), 50–51
Kodokan, 3, 4, 8, 17
Kodokan Black Belt Association, 3
Kodokan goshin-jutsu (kodokan self-defense techniques), 165
Kodokan judo, 1, 3, 4
Kogi, 8
Kogusoku, 2
Koka (almost *yuko*), 157, 158
Koshi Guruma (Hip Wheel Throw), 84–85
Koshiki-no-kata (forms of antiquity), 165
Koshinomawari, 2
Ko-soto Gake (Minor Outer Leg Hooking Throw), 90–91
Ko-soto Gari (Minor Outer Leg Sweeping Throw), 82–83
Ko-uchi Gari (Minor Inner Leg Sweeping Throw), 82–83
Kuchiki-taoshi (Dead-Tree Dropping Throw), 88–89
Kumikata, 2
Kumiuchi, 2
Kyogi, 8
"*Kureba mukae, sareba okuri*" (expression: When opponent comes, welcome him; when he goes, send him on his way), 8
Kuzushi (balance), 16–19
Kyu (lower ramk), 144
Kyushin-ryu (jujutsu school), 2

Lao-tzu, 7
Lee, Bruce, 67
Leg Squats (exercise), 50–51
Leg Thrusts (exercise), 52–53

Locust Posture (yoga), 28–29
Lord of the Dance Pose (yoga), 34–35
Low breathing, 43–44

Mae-ukemi (Front Breakfall), 60–61
Magnesium, 149
Mai-tai (I surrender), 117
Mana, 43
Matte, 158, 169
Meditative poses (yoga), 42
Meiji Restoration, 1, 2, 3
Menkyo (ancient 'licensed' rank), 143
Mid-breathing. *See* Chest breathing
Minerals, 149–50
Mirua-ryu (jujutsu school), 2
Mizu no kokoro (mind like water), 137
Moku-roku (ancient 'cataloged' rank), 143
Morote seoinage. See Seoinage
Mountain Bending Pose (yoga), 32–33
Mudansha (lower ranks), 144
Mushin (no-mind), 137, 138–39
Mushin-no-shin (mind of no-mind), 8. *See also Mushin*
Mutual benefit and welfare (judo's objective), 141

Nage-no-kata (forms of throwing), 164
Nage-waza, 3, 14, 66–115, 161, 162
Ne-waza (groundwork), 117, 155–56
Nogare breathing, 46–47
No-mind. *See Mushin*
Nutrition, 147–153

Ogoshi (Major Hip Throw), 73, 76–78, 104, 110
O-Guruma (Major Wheel Throw), 104–5
Oil of evening primrose, 153
Oku-eri (ancient "entrance to secrets" rank), 143
Okuri-ashi-barai (Double Ankle Sweep), 86–87
Okuri-eri Jime (Lapel Choke), 130–33
Olympics, 4, 5
Osaekomi-waza (holding techniques), 117–21, 157, 159, 165
O-soto-Gari (Major Outer Leg Sweep), 74–77
O-soto-Guruma (Major Outer Wheel), 108
O-soto-Otoshi (Major Outer Dropping Throw), 108–9
O-uchi-Gari (Major Inner Leg Sweep), 78–79

Peacock Pose (yoga), 27
Penalties in contest, 159–60
Perfection (*jikono kansei*), 141
Phosphorus, 149
Plateaus, 136–37
Plow Pose (yoga), 38–39
Posture, 17, 19–21
Prana, 43
Pranayama (yogic breathing), 23, 43–45
Protein. *See* Amino acids
Push-ups, 48–49

Randori, 16, 46, 138–39, 144, 147
Rank, 12
    conversion, 145
    minimum time (chart), 146
Rei (bow), 8, 9, 10–11 (photos)
Renkoho-no-kata (forms of arrest), 166
Rentai-ho, 8
Reishiki (etiquette), 8–14, 165
Restraint breathing, 44–45
Rolling breakfalls, 60, 62–63
Roosevelt, Theodore, 4
Ryu (school), 1, 2, 3, 143

Samurai sword, 2
Sankaku-jime (Triangular Strangle), 132–33
Sasae tsuri-komi-ashi (Lift-Pull Ankle Sweep), 82
Seibukan Association of America, 5
Seigo-ryu (jujutsu school), 3
Seiryoku-zen'yo, 8, 17, 141
Seiryoku-zenyo kokumin-taiiku (a judo kata), 165
Sekiguchi-ryu (jujutsu school), 3, 4
Sensei (teacher), 3
Seoinage (Back Carry Throw), 80–81
Seoi-otoshi (Back Carry Drop Throw), 80–81
Shiai, 144
Shihan, 3
Shime-waza (choking techniques), 117, 126–33, 165
Shintai, 14–15
Shinzentai (natural posture), 19–21
Shobu-ho, 8
Shonen, 144, 145
Shooting Arrow Pose (yoga), 34–35
Shoulder Stand (yoga), 27–28
Shubaku, 2
Sit-ups, 50
Siva Pose (yoga). *See* Lord of the Dance Pose
Slump, 136–37
Sodium, 149
Sogo-gachi (compound win), 157
Soto Maki-komi (Outside Wrapping Throw), 106–7
Sport rules, 154–66
Strategy, 134–39
Sugar, 152–53
Sugar water, 24
Sukui-nage (Scooping Throw), 102–3
Sulfur, 149
Sumi-gaeshi (Corner Throw), 100–101
Sumi-otoshi (Corner Dropping Throw), 114–15
Sun Salute (yoga) 40–41
Sushin-ho, 8
Sutegeiko exercises, 138

Tai Chi Ch'uan, 48
Tai-jutsu, 2
Tai-otoshi (Body Drop Throw), 18, 86–88
Taisabaki (body movement), 3, 14–15 (chart), 16
Takenouchi, Hisamori, 2

Takenouchi-ryu jujutsu, 2
Tan Tien (center), 19
Tani-otoshi (Valley Drop Throw), 70, 100–101
Tao-te-ching (Taoist religious/philosophical text), 7
Tate Shiho Gatame (Vertical Four Corner Hold), 120–21
Tenshin shinyo-ryu jujutsu, 2, 3, 8
Three cultural principles of judo, 8
Tokugawa, Ieyasu, 1
Tokugawa regime, 1, 2
Tomita, Sensei, 4
Tomoe-nage (Circle Throw), 80, 96–97
Torite, 2
Tortoise Pose (yoga), 38–39
Triangle Pose (yoga) 36–37
Tsugi-ashi, 14 (chart), 15
Tsukuri, 14, 19
Tsunetoshi, Ikudo (great *jujutsu* teacher), 3, 16
Tsuri-goshi (Lifting Hip Throw), 90–93
    o-tsuri-goshi (Major Lift), 90
    ko-tsuri-goshi (Minor Lift), 90
Tsuri-komi-goshi (Lift/Pull Hip Throw), 84–85
Twist Pose (yoga), 36–37
Two-man stretching exercises, 52, 54–55

Uchikomi exercise, 138
Uchi-mata (Inner Thigh Throw), 90–91, 104
Ude Garami (Arm Wrapping Lock), 122–23
Ude Gatame (Arm Crush), 122–23
Ukemi-waza (Breakfalls), 56, 58–65, 147
Uki-goshi (Floating Hip Throw), 72, 75, 110
Uki-otoshi (Floating Drop), 106–7, 108
Uki-waza (Floating Technique Throw), 100
United States Judo Association (USJA), 4, 144
United States Judo Federation, 4, 144, 146
Ura-nage (Rear Throw), 112–13
Ura-ukemi (Rear Breakfall), 58–59
Ushiro-goshi (Rear Hip Throw), 112–13
Ushiro Kesa-gatame (Rear Scarf Hold), 118–19
Ushiro Sankaku-jime (Rear Triangular Strangle), 132–33

Utsuri-goshi (Change Hip Throw), 104–5

Vitamins, 150–52
    A, 150
    B complex, 150–51
    C, 151
    D, 152
    E, 152

Waki-gatame (Arm Pit Hold), 126–27
Wa-jutsu, 2
Water, 152
Waza-ari (half-point), 157, 158
Weight training, 138
Wheel Pose (yoga), 39

Yagyu Tajime-no-kami (great samurai), 137
Yamashita, Sensei, 4, 94
Yang, 7, 8
Yawara, 2
Yin, 7, 8
Yoga Breathing. *See Pranayama*
Yoga Postures. *See Asana*
Yoko Gake (Side Hooking Throw) 114–15
Yoko-guruma (Side Wheel Throw), 110–11
Yoko-otoshi (Side Drop), 92–93
Yoko Shiho-gatame (Side Four Corners Hold), 120–21
Yoko Wakare (Side Separation Throw), 110–11
Yoko-ukemi (Side Breakfall), 58–61
Yoshin-ryu (jujutsu school), 2
Yudansha (upper belts), 144
Yuko (almost *waza-ari*), 157, 158

Zanshin (fighting spirit), 14
Zarei (Kneeling Bow), 9, 10
Zen, 2, 8, 136, 137
Zempo Kaiten Ukemi (Forward Rolling Breakfall), 62–65